PURE BULL
—WELL ORGANIZED

Bob Schild

With An Introduction By
Hal Cannon

Illustrations By
Mike Stanger

Distributed By:
B Bar B Leather
719 W. Pacific
Blackfoot, Idaho 83221
(208) 785-1731

Copyright © 1996 by Bob Schild
Illustrations © 1996 by Mike Stanger

All Rights Reserved. This book, or parts thereof
may not be reproduced in any form
without permission in writing from the publisher.
Printed In The U.S.A.
by The Printery, Blackfoot, Idaho

Library of Congress Cataloging-in-Publication Data
Schild, Bob
Pure Bull -Well Organized : Cowboy Poetry, Folklore,
Western History
ISBN 0-9616569-1-3

TABLE OF CONTENTS

Introduction, Getting it Right	i
PREFACE	iv
THE PRESUMPTUOUS ROOKIE	1
COLLEGE COWBOY	2
THE COWBOY, PASSING OF A LEGEND	5
DOCTOR BILL (Larsen)	7
THE ROOT OF ALL EVIL	11
A NOSE IS A NOSE IS A NOSE	13
THE POVERTY WAGON	15
HAPPY BIRTHDAY BOB (PETERSON)	17
OWEN BARTON, COWBOY POET	19
COWBOY POETRY, CREATION & CONTENT	21
WHOA UP, SANTA	23
THE IDAHO SPUD	25
INSTINKED	27
TOP OF THE WORLD	29
THE TIE	35

FRIENDS NEED FRIENDS	37
TRAINING OLD BLUE	39
RERIDE	41
THE GREY WOLF	42
THE FIVE SEASONS OF THE YEAR	45
LOVE IS A BLOOMER	47
POLLY-TICS	49
CARIBOO MOUNTAIN MURDERS	52
AMBUSHED	69
CHRISTMAS AT GRANDMA'S	71
THE GOOD LIFE	73
HARRY	75
HOOTIE	79
THE BUTTON AND THE CHAMP	82
RIDE FOR NINETY-ONE	85
THE LONG RIDE	86
TOM, DO YOU REMEMBER?	88
THE JAM O'R JERRY'S ROCK	91

LOSS BREEDS LONESOME	*95*
THE MAVERICK BULL	*97*
LUCK	*99*
LIGHT THE BOARD	*100*
UNCLE PAUL	*103*
SOCK IT TO HER AL	*105*
RODEO JUDGE	*109*
GRACIAS AMIGOS	*110*

INTRODUCTION, GETTING IT RIGHT
BY HAL CANNON

When we started the Cowboy Poetry Gathering in 1985, Bob Schild was one of a handful of poets who came to recite poems about rodeo. I've always admired anyone who attempts to capture in language something that defies language. Rodeo is not easily put into words. Rodeo is full of emotion -- fear and courage. Rodeo is visual - full of kinetic action. Rodeo is historical - anyone involved in rodeo is full of stories about the past, about the characters and calamities that chronicle the sport.

Besides the power of his poems, two things stick out about that first encounter with Bob Schild. I asked him why he learned cowboy poetry. Remember, this was long before cowboy poetry became popular. Few cowboy poets had published books and this was before there were scores of cowboy poetry events to perform at. Bob told me he and his buddies learned poems to keep each other awake on those long all-night drives between rodeos. I loved that foundation of poetry appreciation. The old poems were not learned to impress anyone. Their function was just part of life, staying awake.

The other thing Bob told me, which always stuck with me, is how when he writes a poem his main attention is to "getting it right." I often asked myself what does Bob mean by this ? What does it take to get a poem right? I know that if you could catalog the ingredients of what Bob does to get a poem right you would have captured the qualities of his poetry.

A partial list might include: Bob is true to the memory of his friends and to the experiences they shared. His poems reflect the past as accurately as possible. Bob has lived the life,"first hand." He knows the fear and courage of the eight second ride. Though it takes digging deep in the soul, Bob finds words to express the emotions of a life lived on the line. Bob chooses a full range of experiences to express in poetry. His poems go from a heart wrench to a belly laugh. Bob is a craftsman. He gives the same attention to the traditional craft of rhyme and meter that he would give to the working of leather into a fine saddle.

It is said that only about 5% of the garden variety fruits and vegetables that were commonly grown a hundred years ago are being grown today. What happened to those ninety-five percent of varieties that are lost? Did we decide that five types of apples sold in the supermarket represent the best taste and texture? Did we not need the other types of apples? We believe because there are a hundred channels to choose from on TV that our choice is vast. We have gained many things in the past century but what have we lost?

Bob Schild is one of those rare varieties that they just don't raise anymore. His poems represent a community memory of rodeo and ranch life which is passing out of existence.

The community memory I am writing about is not the fact that Bob can recite fifty poems from memory. It is that memory which Bob holds and expresses in his poetry that tells what rodeo was about when Bob won the Saddle Bronc at the N.I.R.A. finals in Portland, 1952. It is the memory of traveling the professional rodeo circuit during the fifties and sixties. It is the memory of all the stories told over a saddle making bench at his shop, B-B Leather in Blackfoot, Idaho. It is the heritage of southern Idaho. This memory is a treasure and what makes it a treasure is that Bob is not stingy with that memory. He puts all his energy and talent into words, verses and poems. He gets it right for us..

This is Bob's Second collection of poetry, his first being, Spur Tracks and Buffalo Chips. His poems have appeared in numerous anthologies including a best selling anthology I compiled in 1986, Cowboy poetry, A Gathering.

For this collection he is joined by an old musician friend of mine who is a top hand artist and illustrator, as well. Mike Stanger grew up in southern Idaho on the Double Arrow Ranch near Idaho Falls. He has illustrated three other books, has made custom western paintings for Gibson Guitar Company, and his works can be found in galleries in Idaho and Montana.

    Hal Cannon
    Founding Director
    Western Folklife Center, Elko Nevada

PREFACE

The old west is gone but not deceased. It lives forever in the hearts, minds, novels and poetry of those who savor its culture and its memory.

Being myself creatively, socially and emotionally involved, as a contributing Cowboy Poet, has afforded me the opportunity to overhear and partake of the usually friendly debates on basic whys and wherefores of Cowboy Poetry – What constitutes a cowboy and who has a license to authoritatively represent the breed?

There are, in my opinion, no justifying requirements, no limits, no rules. Cowboy poetry of today seldom bears the scent of chuck wagon grub or the dust of a trail herd plodding from Brownsville, Texas to Browning, Montana, nor does it describe the weary thud, thud of horses hooves on prairie sod at the close of a days or weeks long journey - guided only by stars, mountain ranges or river drainages. We, for the most part, are observers whose deepest roots may scarce touch upon a now faded past.

Growing up on a farm livestock operation on the edge of the Fort Hall Indian Reservation, I, from my earliest recollections, have considered myself a cowboy, who has at every stage of life been affiliated with livestock people. Educated a stockman (B.S., Animal Science, Colo. A. & M. College), I performed as a rough string rider (or modern day equivalent thereof) continuously for over eighteen years, riding saddle broncs, bareback broncs and bulls-from the Cow Palace, in San Francisco to Madison Square Garden in New York City (competing full time eight of the eighteen). I won the "National Intercollegiate Rodeo Assn." titles in Saddle Bronc and Bareback Riding (in 1954) and currently hold a Gold Card (lifetime) membership in the PRCA (card # 4830).Thirty three years of my life were spent running my own successful saddle shop (B Bar B Leather) in Blackfoot, Idaho. I know no other life than that of the rancher, horseman & rodeo cowboy. The language, the mannerisms, the warmth, the humility and appreciation for humor are the wonderful traits, that abound in these, my truest friends! This facet of life my verse reflects.

Cowboy poetry has many definitions. My own: It is generally easy to understand and its scope is endless. Cowboy Poetry, as I see it, consists of thoughts or opinions expressed freely, in verse, that portray an unbridled western life of today and yesteryear from numerous, varied points of view. No one has the right to qualify or censure it.

DEDICATION

This book is dedicated to the friends and family who have taken that final ride into eternity. They are sorely missed and shall be forever remembered.

THE PRESUMPTUOUS ROOKIE

    Many of my best friends are or have been police officers. This poem is not intended to reflect on them or any of the other personable representatives of law enforcement.
    Within the trade it is called "The John Wayne Syndrome". I would exemplify the classification as a policeman who arrests his own grandmother, handcuffs her, puts her in the squad car, and drives her to the police station. Then he books her for jaywalking at a street dance.
    Rodeo cowboys, on their way to a distant rodeo, usually allow their speed to be limited only by the length of their accelerator pedal stem. We've all had at least one encounter with a "P.R..."

I drive a cop-car when I'm pinned to a star,
For my name is "Officer Bristol."
I get ego kicks watching "Dick Tracy" flicks.
I'm huge when I'm strapped to a pistol.

I'm really quite sage, for a peacock my age,
So don't think that I'm only braggin'.
I'm no common boob, I'm like one on the tube,
The officer called "Festis Hagen."

I watch the girls pass, when I'm shined up like glass
And urged by a pulsating spigot.
I'm macho, by gar, when I leap from my car
And threaten to give them a ticket.

I'm here to admire, like side-walls on a tire,
important as nuts in the dressing.
Agile as a deer, I can kiss my own rear,
Now see why I'm so damned impressing!

COLLEGE COWBOY

"Damn son, get up, " my pappy roared.
"You'll go through life a fool.
Heads should do more than sport a hat.
They function as a tool --
When plans to glean the fruits of life
Are rooted in the school.
Don't waste your future snortin' girls
And chalkin' up for pool."

Pop flanked me down and hosed me off.
He roached my tousled mane;
Sent two Blue-Dogs to load me in
The belly of a train.
It whisked me from the rural life
To one much more urbane --
Then spilled me at an institute
That fertilizes brains.

The best prof's in the business sought
To cultivate my mind.
'Til therein flourished intellect
And manners well refined.
Perhaps they thought I'd graduate
More artfully inclined.
But educating cowboys is
A craft yet undefined.

Did I crack the books? I crushed them!
Why this was apple pie.
All my instincts, at the moment,
Said, "Pump this college dry!"
When I'd milked it maxi-limit --
And this you can't deny --
I'd wrest' each opportunity
With good old "College Try!"

Then I heard a distant calling --
A destiny with fate:
To ride rank bulls and horses from
Behind a numbered gate.
Those gilded books and Ivied Halls
Seemed somehow second rate.
The gifted words of Shakespeare could
No longer penetrate.

When Dad-Time closed winter quarter
Spring's fragrance cast its spell.

I'd rub rosin on my bull-rope
To listen to its bell.
And the field of academics
I farmed no longer well.
But shifted my attention in
Directions I shall tell.

From this point forward into life
The Anthem's fading strains
Gave way to: "Cinch your riggin's boys.
The money's in their manes!"
Then came that rush - Adrenalin –
Coursing Athletic veins.
How sweet the smell of victory
That brings financial gains!

No, fame did not deny me
Upon that dusty trail --
When outlaw horses pitched their best --
Though some did "pack the mail".
Still "Brahmertitis" could set in
If buck turned to impale.
It's strange how fleet a cowboy's feet
With horns prodding his tail.

Yes, I've heard the grandstands rumble
Like distant thunder claps.
I've driven multitudes of miles;
Worn out a thousand maps.
Now I'm facing life "Age-Foundered,"
Much wiser too perhaps.
But the beans that blunt my hunger
I earn by building chaps.

THE COWBOY, PASSING OF A LEGEND

His legs warp in the middle;
Sorta rounded at the knees.
How he walks? Now that's a riddle —
On human parenthesis.
He's ordained to "Cow" a little;
Can't deny, on stems like these.
Ain't a jack-knife meant to whittle?
Don't a bird-nest fit in trees?

He's gnarled as scattered driftwood
Washed upon a sandy shore;
Indicating hardship withstood
In a life of range-rapport.
His scars he flaunts like knighthood.
He won't ever ask for more.
He's cultured them since boyhood;
'Cause he's cowboy to the core!

Some love the stilted fable;
Try, in vain, to be a part.
They saddle poor "Old Mable"
With more gear than she can cart
And dress, near as they're able,
In duds called fashion-smart.
But — damn the glowing label!
They ain't cowboy in their heart!

The cowboy legend's fading
And but a few folks understand —
Not while Hollywood's degrading
His romance with cows and land —
An' city-folks parading —
As they tell — "to call his hand!"
That's sinful promenading;
For they just can't read his brand!

DOCTOR BILL (LARSEN)

Gosh Tex, it would be sumthin'
Fer tuh ace thuh social swim,
Thuh ladies all ignore me,
But they mob young Curly Jim.
Ah wear muh newest britches
An smear goose-grease in muh hair,
Rub clover in both arm-pits
An muh long red underwear,
Them purites still avoid me,
Like I'm droppin's frum a bear.

"Joe, holy rollin' Tony,
All yer molars look a fright,
Like snags cut in a punkin,
Lit on Jack-o-Lantern night.
Yer puss ain't sex-appealin',

With a Jack-Saw fer a smile,
There's them cud make sum changes,
An' so help yer luck a pile.
Don't sit out here a-sulkin,
Give tooth-doctor Bill a trial."

"Doc Bill's a cowboy dentist,
Why I trust 'im like mu hoss.
He'll free up all yer grinners
Of terbacky-juice an' moss,
An' when thuh job's completed
An' uh square yer whiskered chin,
Roar up in yer ol' pickup
An' yuh flash a frenly grin,
Them gals, when yew go courtin',
Will get crinkles in their skin."

"Doc's ped-ee-gree is proper,
Fer as is explained tuh me,

Thuh 'Law West Of The Pecos'
Decorates his fam'ly tree.
It's said, his mother's uncle,
Was 'the Hangin' Judge,' Roy Bean.
From bred in rangeland thinkin,
Well, he jist ain't apt tuh wean.
His wore-out boots an' Stetson
Are thuh only life he's seen."

Ah slapped muh kack on badger,
An' we hit alope fer town,
Them lonesomes was commandin'
Ah should turn muh life aroun'.
Muh heart wuz geared fer romance,
An' Ah really sweat a lot,
Muh brain kicked up an' bellared
'Bout them lovin' thinks Ah thought.
Yeah, when them sweeties tumble,
Whey Ah'll hug-um on thuh spot.

Ah rolled back on muh haunches
An' Ah forked thet dental chair,
Thuh miracle a-waitin'
Fer muh kisser thuh repair.
Ah certain never figgered
On regret tuh claim a share,
Ner boot-tracks on thuh ceilin',
An' Ah knowed who put 'em there,
Muh chewers duckin' dallies
Thet wuz throwed with hosses hair.

Then things got right out western
When Ah come down off thet trip:
Doc's purty-smellin' helper
Went an' snared muh upper lip.
A hoss-vet needle rammed me,
Deep enuf tuh prod muh toes,
Ah guess thet's why she twitched me:
Stop muh rarin', Ah suppose.

Ah fought tuh git muh bearin's,
But muh whole durn head wuz froze.

Doc's fingers, wrists an' elbows
Was all plugged intuh muh face.
He shore had set his mind up,
All them notches tuh erase.
He bored jist like a miner,
When thuh ore is exter deep,
Smoke wuz curlin' off his drill,
Like a brush-fire cookin' sheep,
Chain chewin' on muh mustache,
Ah wuz skeered tuh pop a peep.

Then, when thuh scuffle ended
An' Ah stumbled tuh muh feet,
Muh smile, Doc said, wuz "polished
Like a well-rode saddle seat."
It didn't cost no money,
All Ah done wuz X muh name,
Gol durn, it an't yet Christmas,
But thuh feelin's jist thuh same,
Exceptin', when it's Christmas,
Sometimes Red-Eye gits thuh blame.

Ah brought a lookin'-mirror,
Fer tuh practice up muh grin,
'Til muh movie-idol smile
Makes them ladies heads tuh spin.
One look plumb flipped muh gizzard,
Like a sack a drownded pups.
Ah should uh said more no-sirs,
'Cause, respondin' tuh muh yups,
Thet dad-balmed Iv'ry Merchant
Went an soldered all muh cups.

Jack Mitchell Enjoying The Cowboy Life

THE ROOT OF ALL EVIL

"Rodeo's the way to go," said Wyo. Clint one day.
"Yankton trail, this time we fail to earn one dime in pay."
Kremmling Jack said, "Check our sack, we've clearly run our luck."
Loveland Jim, obliging him, says, "Here's one lonely buck.
This is class, we're filled with gas, a full six-pack you know.
Check our speed; why all we need is one more rodeo."

"No, you see it's griping me, this greedy quest for cash.
For," asked Jack, "Why break your back; our life's a nervous rash.
Here's the cause, this buck's the boss; it owns us don't you see?
Have no fear; the end is near, see boys I'll set us free.
We're more wise than many guys; I'll end this evil fight."
This to gain, rolled down the pane and fed it to the night.

    This poem was written especially for my old pard, Jack Mitchell, after an evening of reminiscing in Kremmling, Colorado on January 11, 1990. Jack is gone now --- Rest in peace.

Mount up to show your old horse who's the boss;
You return walking, then you've lost the toss.

A NOSE IS A NOSE IS A NOSE

Time tempers friendships to withstand the test,
Long as true hearts pound away in the chest.
Hose Nose an' Bugle were comrades so blessed,
Ridin' wild hosses is what they did best.

How could such pardners as these come to blows:
Honest contention, in fun I suppose.
Each man defending the size of his nose,
Questions of which was the largest arose.

Both bore the ribbing much better than most,
Deflecting efforts by two pals to roast;
Razzed one another, pretending to boast,
Saluting, in turn, with "Super-Nose" toasts.

Often such chidings, in time, take their toll,
Top pecking order a subconscious goal.
Prevailing hecklers must relish the role.
Dominant natures establish control.

Hose Nose said, "Bugle, your ant-eater face
Easy could suck up each bug in this place,
So huge, your Honker, a human disgrace,
Need not grow longer to sniff outer space."

"Look here," said Hose Nose, your face telescope
Might become famous, just teach it to rope.
Bred I a race horse, I'd opt for one hope:
Flared nostrils like yours — to win at a lope."

Some men, enduring emotional pain,
Crack in the middle from pure mental strain;
Yielding to pressure that addles the brain,
'Til but a shell of the man may remain.

Hose Nose ripped Bugle as never before.

His hard-ridden victim could bear nothing more.
Sensing he never would even the score,
Bug'e found the answer he'd been looking for.

He made arrangements with surgical guys
To beat the problem by shrinking the size.
They carved out a chunk from below his eyes,
Remodeled his snoot to loveable size.

"Feast your eyes Hose Nose 'cause this time I win.
My nose looks better, It's petite an' thin."
Short lived his rapture an' down fell his chin.
Undaunted, Hose Nose requested the skin.

Eagerly Bugle rushed into the trap,
Unthinking, quickly, as fresh from a nap,
"Give you the skin, Hose, you block-headed sap.
How could such nonsense all come from one yap?"

"Old Pard, I figured, when they closed the gap:
That left-over skin, if windy, would flap.
Friendship considered, well I thought perhaps:
With your permission, I'd build me some chaps."

Doubt the story? I suppose. Ask Eddie Quade, that cowboy "nose."

**Disgusting: when some horses eat, they slobber quite a bit.
An old cowboy has found a cure: just teach the nag to spit.**

THE POVERTY WAGON

I stopped to chin with Rancher Jim,
Do some old fashioned blowing.
He'd pop a grin then yarns he'd spin,
With wisdom, wit, and knowing:
Tales of the sky, the mountains high,
where grass of green was showing.
His words came slow, his voice rang low,
Almost like cattle lowing.

At times he'd dwell on jobs done well,
His practiced craft bestowing,
Then scratch his rump and show the pump,
That kept cool water flowing.
And out a way, his home-made sleigh,
He fed with when it is snowing.
There's sheds he's built, with sunward tilt,
For colts, well bred and glowing.

We focused on the two-hole John,
Where flapped the rooster crowing;
To stake his claim on fleeting fame,
For Auburn chicklets growing.
What next I spied reason defied...
An old Ford he'd been towing.
It had no wheel to turn its keel,
To guide its "to and frowing."
The seat was gone one rests upon,
While driving on or slowing.

I says, "By jing, who drives this thing,
Or are there oars for rowing?"
He said, "I know such puzzles grow,
And this ain't bull I'm throwing.
Its owners crass, he's lost his 'rear'
And don't know where he's going."

It's still up there, on "Blue Creek Ranch," near Dubois, Idaho.

HAPPY BIRTHDAY BOB (PETERSON)

You sure ain't much decayin',
For a man of fifty years.
But, profile-wise, you've prospered,
Plus, you've roaned above the ears.
Yet, Pal, the sparkle's stayin',
It's near always in your eye ---
Though just a wee bit faded;
It still glimmers, if you try.

One thing old age can't alter
Is your springboard, youthful step.
It's still as spry as ever ;
If you'll muster up some pep.
What worries me 's a pallor,
Looks like jaundice of the brow ---
The shade, though, looks right healthy;
In the milk of Jersey Cows.

You sure ain't lost your water;
Seems you're always on a trip.
That string there on your finger
Still reminds you to unzip.
If sometimes you feel puny;
Fret thee not, things could be worse.
Pure confidence surrounds you.
That so? "Terry booked a hearse!"

Friend, think strong when you're feelin',
Like a well used Thunder Mug.
Those Blah-h-h s that keep you reeling,
When you're bit by Earpy-Bugs,
Are easy to contend with ---
Get your butt up out of bed.
Pal, swill a snort of Barn Spray
And those bugs are instant dead!

Next fifty years are tougher.
We get harder to repair.
Your upstairs keep in order;
Never yielding to despair.
Hope rides the far horizon;
Though I've never met the man.
"Kill or Cure" 's his motto.
He is called "Kovarkian."

Sure hate to miss the Blow-Out;
For to celebrate your night.
My only contribution
Is to see you're feeling right.
Wise words might aid the effort;
But, for cowboys, talk comes hard.
Forget your damned old wrinkles ---
Have a happy birthday, Pard!

THE SMOKING TRACK
It's the trail of an elk, or track of a deer;
Which of these elusives are you drawing near?
Find twelve sticky droppings, place these in your mouth.
Now arch your neck slowly, first northward then south.
That's all there is to it; if pieces still fit,
You're stalking a deer, so now you can spit!

OWEN BARTON, COWBOY POET

When some future generation turns back a page in time
They'll find a stalwart cowman who's inscribed his life in rhyme.
His style of country living blazed its trail across the page,
For quiet, pensive study in a distant, urban age.

They'll find a western heaven that prevailed here on the earth,
A tired old cowman's pleasure, as he helps a cow give birth,
The dust that trails the roundup of the cattle in the fall;
The trials and perseverance of the folks who love it all.

There's "Don, The Jackass," braying his lusty mating song,
Some hearts might feel the story and a few might bray along.
They'll sense the earth's vibration, as he finishes his tune;
Know loud, impassioned crooning is a sign he wants to spoon.

They'll learn why "That Old Stetson," settled tightly on his brow,
Was vital to his living as the growing of a cow,
Not just a western fixture that adorns a cowman's head,
To turn the smiles of ladies, but a tool to him, instead.

Perhaps they'll grasp the humor in the busy "Red Ant Hill,"
See something more than torment, but I doubt that many will.
You can't blend pain with humor and expect them to agree
That mirth may sooth the injured, though it works for you and me.

"The Early Morning Roundup" sure might leave their heads awhirl.
But they won't think it's cowboy, with no guitar and no girl.
They won't see dapper heros, always riding at a lope,
But just a dusty cowman, with a cow-horse and a rope.

They'll miss a heap of pleasure, but they won't understand,
A kind that's never known, until you shake his calloused hand.
No, they'll never share that feeling, like most of us have done;
'Cause time has carved his notches on the handle of its gun.

If they've read the pages proper they'll feel the evening breeze.
They'll know he's still among them, with a horse between his knees.
They'll know his cows are milling, when the night-winds groan and fuss.
And they'll know his mind's at peace now, just like the rest of us!

COWBOY POETRY
CREATION & CONTENT

My booted pards had gathered.
Sure, they speculate a lot;
Concocting doubtful versions
Of the fame their twines had brought.
Some, headin' – heelin' grizzlies,
Fearful nay of fang nor claw;
Their artful cowboy legends
Mostly products of the jaw.

We heard from "Long-rope-Louie".
Say, he chattered like a squirrel.
His exploits topped the boasters
And his grit impressed his girl.
He scoffed at barren deserts,
Rode the mountain's craggy tips.
'Twas mighty near tomorrow
'Fore he stilled his flapping lips.

I took my turn at chinning
My contrived, creative best,
Relating to the culture
Brought by cow-folks to the west.
I'd cracked a bunch of "good-uns,"
Meant to entertain the group,
By sharing of the action
Known to feed a hungry loop.

I spied a scowling lady ---
Like a ghoul from hell possessed;
A female Doubting Thomas,
Who was plainly unimpressed.
She blocked my verbal aces
With intimidating stare ---

That bored right through my Wranglers
To my ragged underwear.

She raved, "Must every cowboy
Spew such nonsense when he talks?
Your verse, by scent and content,
Matches droppings from an ox.
Excessive in your telling;
You exaggerate a lie ---
Whose reeking barnyard smelling
Would repulse a stupid fly!"

Now you know why I should seek
To blunt her rude impression,
To cast out the shade of doubt
She placed on our profession.
Scholars you, who share her view,
Stand thee henceforth, well-advised:
Bluntly put, cow-poetry
Is, "Pure-Bull, well organized!"

When Eagles suffer gas pains
(They often do I've heard),
In ancient Indian Legend,
They're called,"The Thunderbird."

WHOA UP, SANTA

Ding blast your old hide, Santa,
Get those prong-ox off my roof;
It's not for fancy prancin'
By a herd of cloven-hoof.

It's time that you quit grazin'
On those goods beneath the tree.
You're packin' too much belly
And that grub belongs to me.

Yeah, I've heard scads of stories:
How you stopped to share your poke.
Your brand of socializing
Tends to keep this cowboy broke.

Hey, where's your little woman,
While you race across the sky,
With nose as red as Rudolph's?
It's no wonder you both fly.

Now learn to mind your manners,
Either drive or park that sled.
Then I'll be much obligin'
And I'll go on back to bed.

Politicians balance budgets? Well that promise isn't new.
The surest way to do it is to export quite a few.

THE IDAHO SPUD

On a picture-perfect ev'ning,
    When the Autumn Moon is high
And the world is locked in slumber,
    'Neath a star-laced, endless sky,
When a billion tiny tubers
    Leave their beds of sand to play,
It's in joyous preparation
    For next graduation day.

When the moon smiles merry moonbeams
    At the spectre in the night,
To a tinkling, silent music,
    As delightfully it might,
Each potato proudly gyrates
    To the rhapsody it hears,
Ev'ry dancer feels the music,
    For potatoes have no ears.

They absorb a night air fragrance
    From their prance upon the rows,
And it's all for human pleasure,
    For potatoes have no nose.
No one ever hears a footstep,
    As they rumble to the beat.
It is not a mystic silence,
    'Cause potatoes have no feet.

Then the rapture of the moment
    Fades away as it began,
When each Idaho Potato
    Dons a coat of russet tan.
One and all fits to perfection,
    Like a custom underwear –
Sure is welcome each September,

Cont.

For potatoes have no hair.

In the light of early dawning
    Young potatoes seek their beds;
Where a sandy, fluffy pillow
    Insulates each russet head.
Here's a fact I've often pondered:
    Still a mystery to me,
Though tubers share a trillion eyes,
    No potato, yet, can see.

Most Bakers end their ev'ning
    In a manner dignified,
But some others search for trouble
    And they end up getting fried.
Many miss their homeward calling,
    Like, so often, humans do,
Then seek to bunk most any place,
    There's no potato stew.

It's time that the cowman break free from the chain
Which keeps him from earning fair profits again.
For even a sea gull, buoyed only by luck,
Can place a deposit upon a new truck.

INSTINKED

In-stinked, I'd call it, at least let's suppose.
Cowboys shed fingers but never a nose.
"Cowboyin' Culture", that name's the reward
For earnin' one's keep a-straddle "Old Pard."
Proud of his calling, he's somewhat aloof.
Frost-bound, he's horseback, when snow blasts his roof.
He'll ride in the night, a cow-huntin' hoss:
In four feet of snow, at whim of the boss.
Cold fingers grow stiff, then burn at the tips
And frost makes a smile plumb shatter blue lips.
A northern might crop the tip of one ear;
His only warm spot, a well hidden rear.
Ice nips off fingers. It blackens the toes.
Never a cowboy will freeze off his nose.

The reason, I've found, is part of his creed.
When facing tough times he turns to his steed.
It ain't a secret why those frosty paws
Freeze off a cowboy, but never his schnauz.
Most every cowboy is smart as he looks,
He'll never rely on survival books.
Any wise waddy will use his cayuse
To fend off the cold, His pipes dripping juice.
Now here's what he does, down-wind from his hoss,
When gales up his snout blow frosty an' cross;
Displacing the tail, he roots under there,
Where close to the skin, a hoss has no hair.
He presses 'er deep, with a face-saving flair,
Prays for expulsion of nose-warming air.

Untrue, of course. This particular fabrication came about during the razzing of a friend who happened to be missing his right thumb but sported a somewhat prominent olfactory bulb. Sorry, I can divulge no names.

TOP OF THE WORLD

Race-blood sires a winner, by limited share.
The rest of the package is wrapped in the mare.
Review her potential by greats she's undone.
Genetic prepotence is proved by the son.

A bold dash to glory, back some years ago,
Began with a filly and Pro-Rodeo.
When she whip-lashed the string she reset the clock,
Then headed the fleetest Coriente stock.

Her pedigree royal, those credits were fine.
She'd gallons of blue-blood back to the third line.
Enriching each movement ... grace, nimble and quick,
All pluses, no minus, somewhere there's a niche.

Pride dominates pleasure in horses that can,
Both mine and her owner, a fast-loop Sho-Ban.
Spoke he, "All my people love fast running steeds,
But now, we're much wiser, no trading for beads."

In life there are moments when man sets his sights
So high on the spectrum he can't sleep for nights.
Might then be he tempted to dig extra-deep,
Or, damn human weakness, return home and weep.

I'll lay it out plain, you may think as you please ...
That fast stepping mare bent my pocket three g's.
There's no wheeler-dealing. The kid's pretty tough.
For certain, one Sho-Ban knows how to swap rough.

Don't let it be said, "I've regretted the move."
Whatever the calling, she mastered the groove.
When they rang the bell and popped open the gate ...
It's "So long for now, boys, she won't hesitate."

She fit all the aspects in horse racings game.

So Grey Elk, the speedster, dashed onward to fame.
Each sprint down the track lined my pocket with tin.
She made it a habit. The mare lived to win!

The movement of hands in the tic-toc called time
Does vary the course of our dreams so sublime.
And there came a time when this fine Grey Elk mare
Must pass on her speed to the limbs of an heir.

The swiftest of horses do honor their class.
This is not a feature of all who might pass.
But man built processors by which he computes,
Then breeds mares like Grey Elk to speed-machine brutes.

They're countless, the hours spent on books and speed charts,
Selecting breed facts fed to those humming parts.
Approval beamed downward by yon' blinking star,
I bred the mare, Grey Elk, to old Grizzly Bar.

The fetus developes as down burns the wick.
Doubt gnaws at the conscience, contesting the pick.
Smooth as refrains drifting from one Lawrence Welk,
God blessed the deliv'ry of Young Grizzly Elk.

The colt was a wonder and not a whit less.
He showed us the best of both sides, I'll confess.
Born black as the night, so we'll all see the day,
His coat will shed off to a rich dapple grey.

With proud, gentle care and good luck in the plans,
One beautiful yearling stood full fourteen hands.
In fear of the hazards that could end it all,
I built for that youngster his own padded stall.

Consider the dangers of life he must pass,
Like diversion of thoughts to oats and green grass.
Perhaps, in elation, he could someday bolt
And wipe out the future of this yearling colt.

Griz' Elk was a super-horse in his own right,
That thought an obsession, when sleeping at night.
Yeah, he won his maiden, not much of a race,
From gate to the wire, at a blistering pace.

The passion in owning a colt such as this
May better the thrill of a young boy's first kiss.
It makes the heart flutter as if it might burst,
And fills man with pride for this athlete he'd nursed.

Practice self-discipline; those in a hurry
Learn jumping the gun just guarantees worry.
And though worry I did, he continued to thrive.
I pampered Griz' Elk to the prime age of five.

I'll have to admit to doing some braggin',
Hooked Griz' Elk and a mate to a damn fool wagon.
We paired him up tough, with a winner to start.
Griz' jack-knifed that fleet-foot back into the cart.

There is no explaining how one buggy ride
Could cause this strange tremor so deep down inside.
Like many proud horsemen, I swallowed the hook,
Set out to match-mate him . The "world" needs a look.

In three past full seasons on flat racing's track,
He's started in front and then added more slack.
In selecting the year I'd pondered it all...
Find, a fleet-footed mate, a challenge to all.

 Blaine Schvaneveldt jingled, called John Cooper too,
In search for the best, 'cause no other will do.
"When you've found the horse and you both can agree...
Odds, fifty are nifty, you'll satisfy me."

I spent many months in the shade of the phone
And waxed therapeutic Griz' Elk's muscle tone.
Then, crowning the hope that had lighted the way ...
"We're shipping your horse. He'll be up there today."

"This gelding's a dandy, he thinks winning's fun.
He's dappled in color, old Grizzly Bar's son.
The scourge of the big tracks, he's set them on fire,
Been winning and grinning from gate to the wire."

Such fine buggy horses few horsemen have seen,
Poetic in motion, a flying machine.
They floated like singles. They sifted the breeze,
Were feared like a death from an unknown disease.

The two scored a win with each crack of the gate.
But we opted for home the week of "The State."
Heat lesions aren't normal, so doctor the spot.
The "World Wide," that contest is tempting my lot.

The week of the big one heaped fame on my greys,
And two hard-running blacks deserved equal praise.
We both did our share of winning that week,
The blacks and greys likewise. We'd both reached our peak.

We dream of the day when life's great winners meet,
Well knowing one champion must suffer defeat.
When shouts of the bettors had hardly begun,
 Thump, clang of the gate saw the four break as one.

Approaching the eighth-pole, the crowd came alive,
For each of the four was increasing his drive.
In this close a horse race there's no room for liars.
Those blacks equaled my greys each step to the wire.

In wait for the photo, the fans stood in shock,
Still clutching their billfolds, declining to talk.
No doubt, it's the closest race I ever saw.
Whatever the angle – the race is a draw.

I'll tell you straightforward, that crowd was uptight.
And damned few among them will sleep well tonight.
The great thing displayed here – formidable try;

Tomorrow both teams will be getting a bye.

We all have the jitters when finals arrive.
And most of the fans have succumbed to the hives.
All forty-three races held out to the wire,
With everyone's thoughts on the last teams to fire.

All horses aligning for race forty-four;
Dead silent and breathless, three thousand or more,
While ev'ry ear listened, gates popped with a crash.
An even-up four-pair had started their dash.

A length from the eighth saw two teams falling back.
But neither team fading is grey nor is black.
Oh man, what a horse race! Just look at them go,
Lined up like four arrows all shot from one bow.

It's known in a horse race there's someone must win,
Though margin be wide or by one very thin.
And never's the horse race that I ever saw,
That twice could four horses run out to a draw.

The gamblers were silent, still gasping for breath.
Lose five or five hundred, it's painful as death.
This word from the judges, that, "Like it or not,
Let's tarry a moment. We'll blow up this shot."

Straight edges and glasses present the same view...
Tips of four noses on lines that they drew.
A dead-heat in horse race...there is no disgrace...
Two damned fine grey horses have won---second place!

THE TIE

The talents of a poet
Don't fit a cowboy's frame.
It takes real school-book learnin'
To play their wordy game.
But Hooter had a yearning
To be a cowboy bard,
Well knowing gold an' glory
Is seldom their reward.

His goal became perfection
Of brilliant lines inferred,
To blend poetic magic,
By cultivating words.
No song-bird matched the music,
Fine verse became his fame.
His new vocabulary
Brought honor to his name.

Hoot loved to flaunt his knowledge,
Made eloquence a game,
His crafting of expression
Put cow-poets to shame.
His mind was overflowing
With educated clips,
So Hooter picked some toughies
To run between his lips.

But like a nervous puncher,
Out pitching to his date:
Hoot's rush to grand oration
Caused "hyper-verbalate."
He began to vocalize
At such a frenzied pace,
His tongue got snarled an' knotted,
Dead-center in his face.

His case required attention,
No time to fuss or fret,
We jumped him in the trailer
An' headed for the vet.

Doc's wealth was clamps an' scalpels,
They fair plugged up the place.
With riches these, plus logic,
He untied Hooter's face.

Now Hooter's name's a symbol,
The best in cowboy verse.
But "twixt" Hooter an' the vet,
Well, Hooter came out worse.
Doc made himself a million
While learning where to pry,
Inventing, in the process,
The John Deere baler tie.

Mary raised a Bummer Lamb,
She bottle-fed the elf.
Voraciously he wagged his tail,
And spanked his eager self.

True love devastates. This is no baloney.
The most certain cure is called matrimony.

FRIENDS NEED FRIENDS

Sometimes, in life, old parts well worn irritate like a cactus thorn,
And bridle paths, now nature-shorn, mark man for ranks of mossy-horn.

Memory is a pleasant crutch, where never pain is felt as such,
And friendship's feel is warm to touch, to pals who's worth is very much.

A backward glance at life replayed, a horse once snatched, a short parade,
A fee duked out for that charade, a puff of dust, that debt was paid.

Match up a horse of equal skill, too proud to quit, too tough to kill,
Who leaves the box with pent up thrill, and bends the string with winning will.

Place a rope in The Master's hand and scratch a score-line in the sand.
He'll fit the noose in fashion grand, to rolling thunder from the stand.

Such dreams help heal a burning scar, an ember tip, one new cigar,
Then gears will shift and the chasis jar; parts will hum like a brand new car.

Not lives nor dreams are near that end, perhaps do less with more pretend.
The message here, I've hoped to send, "We need you, Pard; get well old friend."

                                        To Neil Love.

TRAINING OLD BLUE

In spite of Blue's calling – to chaperon stock,
The bite of a love-bug spun him into shock.
Out on the old homestead, he'd found peace of mind,
With no special yearning for one of his kind,
But flesh and blood creatures share this basic need:
It's called propagation, it starts with a seed.

Say, he's been a cow-dog, a champ ev'ry inch.
The pup's noble breeding stood out in a pinch,
With no though of leavin,' dog-biscuits his pay,
'Til bell-ringin' hormones brought lust into play.
His brain blew all circuits, cow-instinct was gone,
Replaced by another, an impulse to spawn.

Blue's need for a darlin' boiled over last spring.
He dashed about, madly, to answer this "thing."
Hot dreams of courtship, that scorched his poor head,
Made one smitten cow-dog a lover instead.
Frustrations nor anger cold neither detract,
'Til earthy fulfillment concluded the act.

There's no room for pity when duty comes last.
Should life need arranging, then change it and fast!
For self-preservation must come before love,
When Cupid's bow-twangin' gives passion a shove.
With no thought of tear-drops, I whetted my knife,
Intending to alter Blue's mind and his life.

Then up spoke a cowhand who'd been lounging near,
"My friend, your reaction is thoughtless, I fear.
The wise shall believe me, you too, when it's done.
There's much more at stake here than curtailing fun.
Your ruthless extraction, these words are certain:
Though Blue gets the trim-job, leaves you more hurtin'."

"Back off, Pard, and listen, I can't buy your line.
One flick of the jack-knife, and this pooch of mine,
Will give up romancin', return to his job,
Remember his manners, not act like a slob.
I won't have to keep him corralled with a chain.
He'll cover both fences, when cows trail our lane."

"Not so," said the puncher, "there'll be nothing left,
If you but continue this surgical theft.
You'd best cool your temper and fold in your knife,
Consider the changes to your style of life:
No dog, thusly altered, performs worth a 'sic-im',
'Cause he has no place left where you can kick-'im."

I think back to the Tyhee School,
Those mem'ries of the golden rule.
They worked me like a dog-gone mule.
All efforts failed; I'm still a fool.

Work is a four letter word, some folks say.
How does such logic then classify play?

RERIDE

"The old thrill, Bob, still haunts me, ain't washed away by time.
Always I have spent tuh git full measure fer muh dime.
Way back in our younger days the trip was made fer dough,
Now it'a satisfaction. Ah contest 'Senior Pro'.

When them chute-gates rattle, as Brahmas file inside,
Muh heart drives virile hormones throughout muh bones an' hide.
Then Ah lift muh nine-plait rope an' drop the bell across,
Knowin' Ah ain't ready yet tuh grow no dad-blame moss.

Once muh grass-rope's drawed inta its place behind that lump,
They pull the wide-gate open, Ah'm right agin his hump.
Then, come the welcome whistle, Ah'm still aboard that ox,
An' fittin' as if growed there, like man-sized chicken pox.

Ah love that job remainin'... tuh gather up muh coins,
An all for one eight-seconds astride a critter's loins.
See now, what Ah'm sayin' pard, the high is still a fact.
Do ya mean ta tell Big Ben, yer too old fer the act?"

Sorry Ben, age trimmed my wick. That Bovine Waltz is out.
I ain't about to board one, unless... now hear me out;
If I should call your challenge, it's only as I say:
Ev'ry Humpy in the draw milks sixty pounds per day!

THE GREY WOLF

The mournful howl of the gaunt grey wolf
    Thrills, chills the lonely night.
Its echo falls like a bugle call
    On those who bloat his right.
They hear his cry from a distant sky,
    Rebounding penthouse walls;
A non-feared wail on the concrete trail,
    Where no one stakes his all!

'Tis well to gloat o'er a brick-lined moat,
    When safe in a land apart;
A different view from the hardy few,
    Exposed to the ways that are.
The "gallant ghost" is a myth at most,
    Born of the dreamer's heart.
A lovely thought but the truth it's not,
    Except to worlds apart.

The young he'll wrest from its mother's breast;
    Roll in the blood and gore.
He's one who'll kill for a madman's thrill;
    Murder his sole encore.
He'll rip a fawn from its bearer's spawn,
    Preferring tender meat.
The mother's womb, now her new-born's tomb,
    He quits with dying bleat.

The wolf attacks, hunting best in packs,
    Screened by the dark of night.
'Tis better done if he hides his "fun,"
    Like killer-humans might.
For food, for thrill, he is born to kill,
    "Endangered" counts for naught:
The nesting swan or the salmon's spawn,
    The owl who wears the spot.

He won't kill man? We all know he can.
    Please put that thought to rest.
He'll draw no line if the flesh be mine,
    When hunger drives his quest.
With snows ten deep on the mountain steep,
    No morsal to be found,
Like cougar cats from Starvation Flats,
    The Grey Wolf comes to town.

Pet dogs (they're fat) or a pussy-cat
    Might fuel the Grey Wolf's feast.
Though all above need a human's love,
    Wolf-love: the palate greased!
Some shall deny, with an anguished cry,
    As funding fades, no doubt.
Anneal my rhyme in the sands of time.
    For they shall bear me out.

The page of a book is the land of pretend;
Often will please you, and sometimes offend.
Peek in if you have a few hours to spend.

THE FIVE SEASONS OF THE YEAR

Mankind feels delight in the coming of spring;
Heralding blossoms and birds on the wing.
When mountains of grass glow a bright emerald green
And hides of cow-horses take on a bright seen,
When Bluebirds build nests and most mammals give birth,
We feel strange emotions down here on the earth.
When calves, in fear of the creek's flowing ripple,
Comfort themselves with a nourishing nipple;
The cows from the valleys graze into the hills
And well-rested horses test rough-riders skills.
"Old Sol" tips his hat as he takes a fresh stand
And beams rays of sunlight to warm up the land.

When summer responds to the urging of spring
It's hard to believe how much work it can bring.
Those oysters burned brown by a hot branding fire
Keep many a critter from learning desire.
One swift operation caused passion to pass
To thoughts less inspired, like the munching of grass.
The trailing of cow-herds up into the hills
Leaves rope-swinging cowboys to temper their ills.
The sweltering heat from the sun in the sky
Greens grass on the mountains, while valleys burn dry.
When the cold hoary finger of Jack Frost appears;
Range cowboys start tallying proper marked ears.

New traces of white that appear in the hills
Bring fresh autumn breezes and blow in some spills;
For sleepy-eyed cowboys caught napping, of course,
Who tend to ignore how frost propels a horse.
When tallies chalked up in the old record book
Don't quite turn out even, the answer's to look.
A cowhand back-ridin' has frivolous cares;
When watchers don't know that he's out sev'ral pairs.
He's still on the gather, rope hung on his horn,
'Bout like it's been done from before he was born.

When calves have quit bawlin', they're truck-herded east
And women start planning a Thanksgiving feast.

Soon winter arrives with a terrible blast
And feedin's a chore that ain't ever too fast.
The hands in North-Country break hay-bales tight zipped,
Numb from their hands to their mustache, frost tipped.
A frigid hand-ax, chipping ice from the creek,
Is swung by a cowman too damned froze to speak.
The feed-team is grained, there's fresh hay in the shed.
I'd say, "Now it's time that the feeder gets fed."
The pleasure of winter, a wholesome desire;
Sit close to the stove with a cracklin' wood fire.
This sort of ranch living once lasted 'til spring,
But now there are mem'ries a fifth season brings.

A season unknown to astrology's charts
Is found in the corner of cow-people's hearts.
It's nurtured by cowfolks fresh in from the range,
To blossom in Elko in ways that are strange;
When legions of cowboys ride in from the hills
To brighten the city with poetic thrills.
The valley's ablaze ev'rywhere that you look,
With stories extolled in life's range-story book.
There's heartaches, by millions, that follow a cow
And dreams are full-filled by the just knowing how.
A current of joy seems to waft through the air
And those who can't feel it ain't ever been there!

The surging Stock Market is tempting to some,
Who plot and connive in quest for the plum.
In direct opposition to this epilogue,
I'm bowing out now, for I've just sold my hog.

LOVE IS A BLOOMER

I'd saddled up for my first show, the local High School rodeo,
With eager smile and cheeks aglow, romantic thoughts that grow and grow.

On Dad's fine stallion, sleek and proud, my wildest dreams had not allowed
I'd so perform before such crowd, my cowboy heart with pride endowed.

Now should sweet Betsy see me ride and read the warmth I feel inside
(For true love can not be denied), she'll know that mine is bona fide.

Her fragile features seem to glow, so tender she is bruised by snow.
How can she live the life we know? This dainty queen of rodeo.

I'm captivated, in a trance; she is the angel of romance.
How could I ever have a chance with one who melts me by her glance?

She's much too sweet to yield to sin, this tempting maid with milk white skin.
Oh, how I long to someday win this lovely doll, so fair, so trim.

I feel quite sure I've caught her eye. I'll ride her way, but won't go by.
Perhaps this flitting butterfly could lend her heart to such as I.

She's drenched my heart with fear and pain, lest I may not her favors gain.
No way on earth could I explain the thought that cross my fevered brain.

Approaching like a knight of old, I deemed myself a warrior bold;
With thoughts to her my love unfold, my racing heart I bare' controlled.

A sweet refrain, like birds might sing, now caused my very ears to ring,
With rapture like none else could bring; it only happens in the spring.

Her warm hello assailed my ears, my greatest thrill since childhood years.
What happened next increased my fears, and even now the thought brings tears.

Dad's stallion struck a Saddler's pose; I know not why this time he chose.
Those acrid fumes assailed my nose while droplets spattered Bettsy's clothes.

She chopped me down for all to see, degraded as a hound dog's tree,
By angry words she shot at me, "Damn, take him someplace else to pee!

If there is more to tell, Bill Little will have to tell it.

POLLY-TICS

On chill' dark nights when northern lights
Illuminate the sky,
A lawman's form, whipped by a storm,
Lends fodder to the eye.
A hangman's noose, with strands cut loose,
The ghost wears for a tie.
His eyes they gleam a frightful beam,
Like beacons shining high.
On phantoms wings a hoot owl sings,
"For whom had I to die, for who, for who?"

Now let's go back when crime turned slack,
Deterred by Lawman Ed.
The folks all knew, no ill winds blew,
Most crime, in fact, was dead.
But fight for right is often tight,
When vanity is fed.
And so one night two planned, for spite,
To roll the lawman's head.
As if he knew, the hoot owl flew,
While passing by he said, "for who, for who?"

Pride fields a need the weak must heed,
To prove themselves they can.
So "Martin Slick", with "Polly Tic,"
Devised and evil plan:
A lynching mob would do the job,
If winds of fate to fan,
A fitting quirk by which to jerk
Ed to the frying pan.
The hoot owl's call still questioned all,
As once more he began, "for who, for who?"

Promote the lynch was deemed a cinch
For Polly Tic to play.
At times she'd shown how words alone
Could rip one's world away
With brazen haste false words were placed,
Then wags would clack their say.
She stacked it so the tales did grow,
Morality to stay.
When Ed was gone the fix was on,
The owl observed this way: "for who, for who?"

Now Polly Tic has dealt her lick,
This epitaph remains:
"Another's views one may abuse,
In seizing of the reins."
Since "Martin Slick" helped turn the trick,
He shares her ill-got gains.
Before he's done he'd use his gun
To paint more crimson stains.
The owl looked on, how things had gone,
Then sang his old refrain: "for who, for who?"

Enough I've heard, you round eyed bird,
Your time has come to die."
Then while he cursed, a shot-gun burst
Turned violent the sky!
The shot undressed the hoot owl's breast,
As bare as if to fry.
Then word went 'roun', Slick owned the town,
Which no-one would deny.
The lead-stuffed bird, though dead, inferred,
To all who passed him by, "for who, for who?"

On chill' dark nights when northern lights

Illuminate the sky,
A lawman's form, whipped by a storm,
Lends fodder to the eye.
A hangman's noose, with strands cut loose,
The ghost wears for a tie.
His eyes they gleam a frightful beam,
Like beacons shining high.
On phantoms wings a hoot owl sings,
For whom had I to die, for who, for who?"

WHOA DAN

Horsemen would predict: Dan's training might crack;
If freed from the bit, he'd up-end my hack.

While gusts from the north blew bitterly cold,
Spooking my cayuse — a booger to hold,
Dan made a motion to re-coat the road:
He raised up his tail to scatter a load.
Winds of wild fury, the worst since the drouth,
With roguish delight, blew the bit from Dan's mouth.

CARIBOO MOUNTAIN MURDERS

Oft' days of old – tough, harsh and cold – repressed the right to live.
With outlaws rife, man staked his life – there was no choice to give.
If plans were laid, whence crime was made malignant by abuse,
He paid the call. His sudden fall brought death, the hangman's noose!
The doomed may sigh when death stands nigh, effecting great release.
With hope foremost that "Holy Ghost" bestows eternal peace.

This tale, as told, still shakes the bold, though cloaked in mystery.
The dust of time shed by my rhyme goes back a century.
Young Charlie Reed, three days by steed, rode up Mount Cariboo.
Blackfoot behind, he'd set his mind to forging life anew.
Nature's allure, you may be sure, empowers it to hold.
But add to this, expectant bliss, the taint of yellow gold.

Now Old Cap Winn, grey hair grown thin, where hung his hat was home.
He'd scooped and panned on all the land from Wickenburg to Nome.
When he met Reed they both agreed, the finer things in life
Were waiting there; the mountain air preempted pain and strife.
How great it was that they could pause where nature's wonders glowed.
No need need for dough with pleasures so, they'd found their Mother Lode.

When rambled they to camp one day, expounding on their luck,
Time's interlude of solitude was costing not a buck.
Through snow they sloshed, and joked and joshed, on how their fortunes ran.
"There's gold indeed," Cap Winn decreed, "enough for ev'ry man."
Unknown to Cap, another chap o'r-heard their friendly fun.
Ruthless his trade, once said he made his living with his gun.

He had no home, content to roam, to scavenge and deceive.
Served half a hitch before the ditch, went absent without leave.
Now, searching for an easy score, he'd reached the Cariboo.
He'd caught the scent, and born hell-bent, he knew just what he'd do.
This mad-dog-twerp did misinterp' Cap's joyful story told.
The words Cap said imbued his head with lust for yellow gold!

So while they teased, frustrations eased ; he silent stole behind.
Like stalking prey, he trailed all day with mayhem on his mind.
As drew the night, in fading light, a cabin crossed his view.
The rock-hewn home, with earthen dome, meant refuge for the two.
He loitered there, midst cold despair, then knocked upon the door.

Surprised indeed, they offered feed, soft bedding for their floor.

Viewed through time's screen, pause for cuisine enhanced one trip to hell.
For Williams, Frank, gave bestial thanks to those who served him well.
Now I suppose, in deep repose, they dreamed of treasured things,
Of life and love, the stars above, the new each dawning brings.
Call fate to blame, 'tis such a shame, for futures cloaked in grief.
Warm, friendly ways exposed their days to murder and a thief.

That funky man mapped silent plan , purloined prosperity.
His new found friends he'd blast and send into eternity
With lethal shots to vital spots, so quell their memory...
That none reveal his plot to steal their gold, their money tree.
His plans all laid, soft bed well-made, his efforts right on track,
He'd lure Reed out , when morn's about, waste Cap before he's back.

Reed raised his sight to bag a bite, at breaking of the dawn;
A "sometimes" feat, but tough to beat for keeping groceries on.
More salt and flour than they'd devour, by melting of the snow,
·Still left a need for other feed, perhaps a well-fleshed doe.
Loading his gun, preceding sun, Reed set upon the track
To try his luck on doe or buck (a satisfying snack).

Fresh bloomed the day. Sun's warming rays spun a florescent glow.
The glint of light on crystal white lit diamonds in the snow.
Crisp, cool and bright, the frost fiend's might, kept firm his grip on earth.
While Cap, to beat, with crackling heat, fed fuel into the hearth.
The trail grown old, its track long cold, gossip prefabricates.
Why choose the day, that cellar-way? Can only speculate.

Tilting the door sawed through the floor exposed the rungs below.
Cap went there, yes, but why's a guess. In truth, we'll never know.
A treasure hoard could there be stored, a goal perhaps achieved.
The punk inched in, with mocking grin, cock-sure Cap was deceived.
His wood-ax flail struck to impale and split the miner's head.
As flitting by Cap's range of eye, he felled him cold and dead.

Yes, there was more to self-assure, relying on his gun;
He pumped hot lead into Cap's head, then sheathed his brand of fun.
One life destroyed, his hopes were buoyed by dreams of hoarded gold.
Searched wall and ground, but what Frank found was loneliness and cold.
'Twas then the deed began to seed remorseful misery.
Tomorrow, sold by misdeeds, holds its page in history.

For men who kill, profit or thrill, they know no other way.
Why risk a chance, a neck-tie dance? It's easier to slay.
Self-torment grew. Perhaps Reed knew Frank laid old Cap Winn down.
He'd close the book lest Charlie took the message into town.
For if, in fact, Reed guessed the act, might place Frank in the ground.
But wind was right to gain respite, to turn this turn this thing around.

The crash they make when branches break, ice-laden from the trees,
Strikes ears a lot like rifle-shots, if muffled by the breeze.
No cry or shout to foster doubt, should Reed have heard or not;
Frank prayed for stealth, at stake his health, or life if he was caught.
To his delight, the gale in flight must hamper Charlie's ear.
Definitely, might luck decree that Charlie did not hear.

Late afternoon, before the moon, found Charlie back in camp.
Indeed the hunt, to put it blunt, had yielded but the tramp.
"Cap's craving fish to grace his dish," the tale Frank Williams told.
"The venison is overdone, fresh trout my fancies hold.
Cut Cap some slack. He'll soon be back with rainbows in the pan.
He'll find his way, at night or day, as well as any can."

Real sourdough feed improves indeed with java fresh and hot.
Reed bought Frank's tale, then grabbed a pail and blackened coffee pot,
Stooped at the drink, but who would think he'd close his future there?
Frank crept behind, blew Charlie's mind, below his parted hair.
The shot, by heck, struck Charlie's neck, emerged above the eye,
Into the creek, ne'r more to speak, a horrid way to die!

Essential now, the problem: how to camouflage the crime.
In frenzied haste, thoughts poorly placed might end Frank's lease on time.
Facts must be hid or, God forbid, lay bare his treachery.
One small mistake implying fake and good-bye destiny.
Neurotic doubt turned reason out (Some things the blind may see).
To re-arrange for sake of change ... this hints of lunacy

There Charlie lay, life pumped away, face down in waters pink,
It can't be true, this gruesome view. Prelude to move is think!
Dragged by his boots, snow, filth and roots clung to Reed's face and hair.
Replace his shirt (to void the dirt) and sopping outer-wear.
Left as he'd chose for deep repose, to snooze beneath his bed,
So, calm and cool, the world to fool, indeed the man was dead.

A spattered flood of crimson blood now stained Cap's snow-white hair.
The slippery mass as frosty glass, when Frank inched up the stair.
Cap, stiff and stale, hours past life's fail, in death revenge so sweet,
Now seemed to fight his bearer's plight, 'til Frank despised the freak ...
Whose limbs poked out like twigs about abandoned magpie nests.
At last, kerchunk, shoved 'neath his bunk, the dead man lay at rest.

Aligning facts to smoke-screen acts invites in jurors, doubt.
Should same detect clues circumspect, defense is put to route.
Frank's yield to fear: death's blood did smear in blindly reckless flight,
Then scattered trash and fireplace ash, which emphasized his fright.
'Til all was gone, stacked split-wood on concealing corpses two.
Thus, shaking still from horror's chill, obliterate the view.

A gruesome fright looms worse at night, when demons ooze and creep.
Afraid to dream – the camp downstream might sooth Frank's mind for sleep.
Diluting pain, by effort vain – cohering with the lot –
Brought little cheer to ease the fear now bubbling like a pot.
Frank William's phobe, a manic lobe, had overwhelmed his mind.
Frank Glover sat with Johnson, Matt to hear this tale unwind.

"I can't suppress this awful mess. My brain reels in a spin.
Young Charlie Reed I've harmed indeed, puts goose-bumps on my skin.
My sanity's in jeopardy, with blood scenes in my craw.
My soul I'll hock at Eagle Rock, complying with the law.
Now I must go, your raft I'll row, explain the incident.
If you'll permit the use of it, my need is evident."

"Frank, hold a bit, light here and sit, explain the facts to me.
If Charlie's shot, your water's hot as ever it will be.
If he's bad hurt, you bet your shirt he needs attending to.
No, Doc will come, we'll patch him some and hope that he pulls through.
Perhaps Cap Winn can save his skin, at least 'til we arrive.
We'll raft him down the Snake to town, if he'll just stay alive."

"Men, we're too late to keep that date, he's on the other side.
Gun on full cock, I bumped the stock, that's how poor Charlie died.
He passed to me my rifle, see, took care the butt came first.
He'd checked the bore I'd cleaned before, then came the rifle burst.
He fell down dead, shot through the head, collapsed upon the floor.
As I stood by tears filled my eye, for Charlie was no more.

Glove', This gets worse... I heard Cap curse, while groping for an ax.

I, still in shock, too numb to talk, faced first of three attacks.
One sought to block with rifle stock, as well as it would do.
I, when he struck, parried and ducked, my rifle broke in two.
Parts left of it I used to hit Cap low behind the ear.
His threat to shoot tore at my roots. I fired in deathly fear."

"Frank, Cap's dead too? No wonder you desire to quit the place.
We are concerned at what we've learned; which you alone must face.
If they're both dead, it's like you said, now you must pay the price.
Johnson and me will look to see before we give advice.
We'll check the scene. If you speak clean, your story's bona fide.
But if you lie, by noose you'll die, or Glover ain't my name."

Impending night switched off the light. Pitch-dark obscured the trail.
And drifting snow leaped to and fro, resultant of the gale.
No moon did peek to guide the trek, nor look upon the shame,
As if delay would wipe away the crime and still the blame.
Unseen, a track to lead them back, the cabin so reveal.
Oft' split the dark by way of spark, bright struck with flint and steel.

Dim candle light exposed to sight a carnage view of death,
The type of thing that tends to bring a shortness of the breath.
Firewood they shed from off the dead, prostrate upon the floor.
Then sickness hit Frank in the pit, and Matt could stand no more.
Both unprepared, the two men stared upon the gory scene.
Matt tried to hide the lump inside. Frank Glover's face turned green.

It took, for sure, blood, sweat and more to place Cap on his bed.
His tangled form defied the norm, from toe tips to his head.
Bent arms a fright – one left, one right – as if to block attack,
Stiff legs on fold, might have controlled a kneeler tipping back.
They did their best to help Cap rest until some future date.
How long that be? Must wait and see, can only speculate.

Poor Charlie lay asleep, to say, and limber as a rag.
Not stiff and cold, was tough to hold, with him inclined to sag,
Indeed a fight to bed him right, to lay him straight away;
One at Reed's head, next grasped legs spread, the third to hoist the sway.
Dim candle light softened the night, enshrouding men at rest.
These two fine friends had met sad ends. Two more now stand to test.

What next to do? That avenue embark without delay.
The homeward walk diluting shock, emotions might defray.

Two friends were gone, but carry on. What price must Williams pay?
To set the wheels, the doom it seals shall wait for break of day.
Revenge in mind, who's sleep inclined? Not Frank nor Glover, Frank.
 To doze was not the killer's lot. For that, himself could thank.

A news release to Justice Peace, hand-mailed from Cariboo,
Facts in the note Frank Glover wrote; Matt, web-foot, wallowed through.
From Soda Springs sweet justice sings. The J.P. Judge at hand
Conclusions drew ,his point of view: to make a legal stand.
Delayed the date... full ten day wait until the terse reply,
"The law shall move. We don't approve that innocents shall die."

Back home at camp a daily tramp, to re-inspect the scene,
So snowshoe shod, with help from God, endured the wait between.
Then three days past, since Christmas last, five filed to'rd Cariboo.
Ducks in a row fought drifting snow to march the killer through:
Frank Williams third (the lone jail-bird), First Nelson, Johnson two,
Fourth – Glover passed, Sam Sibblets last, lest capture must renew.

Right from the start, Frank Williams' part cast doubts on his pretense.
He tried to hide the fear inside while pleading self-defense.
Once on the move, might he behoove, replan his wild charade.
At impasse now, he must somehow, escape this travelcade.
He'd little chance. A sideways glance would not go unobserved.
But should one show, he'd make a go. This option he reserved.

The snowshoe drive faced twenty-five long miles to Cariboo.
While on that trail, cold, gaunt and pale, all shared one point of view.
None held a hope he'd beat the rope, nor face the charges down...
Thought later found in folks around the streets of Blackfoot town...
They often said, Williams instead, should volunteer his skin,
'Twould aid his aim to clear his name, enhance his chance to win.

Frank hinged all hope on storms to cope, concealing his retreat.
The cloak of night a boon to flight for artists of deceit.
The weary few neared Cariboo, grown weak of heart and eye,
Frost spurred them on. All choice was gone. To fail now was to die!.
Exhaustion drew the five into resourceful need for rest.
They, chilled and weak, struck Taylor Creek. There each dovetailed a nest.

Damp, musty beds, in rotting sheds, foot-warmers by compare,
To twig-lined ice, which may suffice for hibernating bear.
Limbs may be lost to gnawing frost, turned black neath sheets of white...

Each fought harsh cold, curled tight and rolled, the sleepless, fitful night.
Times such as this man fears death's kiss, for life hangs by a thread.
When sleep does come, stiff bodies numb, they yield as drugged near death.

Impending dawn found Williams gone, departed in the night.
It's doubtful he could landmarks see through sky of floating white.
Frank's only map, filed in his cap, recorded on his brain.
He'd never ride a horse outside, if one he could attain.
The storm, as plied, would surely hide the man's departing track.
If he moved on all hope was gone, to bring the scoundrel back.

A willing way survives on stay; respite misfortune brings.
The facts amaze. One dozen days found Frank in Soda Springs.
Beyond a doubt, he'd snowshoed out, a death-defying trudge.
Plus hundred miles through nature's wiles to reach the J.P. Judge.
In need, life seems to bolster schemes, provoked by deathly fear.
Unfooled, the judge refused to budge, to wipe the record clear.

'Twas hopeless plight. Law did indict. The charge was murder one.
From Soda jail decreed no bail. Frank's goose was cooked, well-done.
Long odds he'd bucked to self-induct, thus beat the Jury Grand.
He'd joined the game to clear his name, but over-played his hand.
Should he have fled, might be instead, free as the ev'ning breeze.
To sit in wait became his fate, with cockroaches and fleas.

One paragraph by telegraph had rocked the county seat.
In frontier times crooks faced their crimes where judge and juries meet.
The message fired action inspired lawmen in Blackfoot town.
A posse filed where winds had piled snow deep and soft as down.
At hardy clip, two days the trip, by horse to Soda Springs.
Then two days back had left no slack for discourse, social things.

Wrists lashed behind relieved Frank's mind of any plans to wag.
But to insure his thoughts stayed pure, gave him the slowest nag.
The trail made rough, by flaky stuff, crossed mountains, springs and brush.
Frank oft' implied , to end his ride, "What was the cockeyed rush?"
All trails extend toward an end, this one the Bingham jail.
Frank soon would dwell, in barred Hotel. Please forward all his mail.

A long, dull wait behind the gate, what caused the great delay?
Law snared its man in early Jan. The date was nearing May.
Killings occur. The coroner investigates the deaths,
Evaluates and speculates; what wrought the dying breaths?

One April day Doc shaved away mystic from Cariboo.
Frank's sworn pretense of self-defense was ruled to be untrue.

On May and four, law cracked the door of Frank's prescribed resort.
Led shackled out, heard inspired shout from lawyers of the court.
May eleven, verdict given: convicted first degree.
Not being cleared, as Frank had feared, they could not set him free.
When trial was done, the web well spun, obliged that Frank must die.
"Hanged by the neck, he should expect," spoke those who testified.

Hays' court adjourned, felt council earned a license to appeal.
One final try to reach blue sky, High Court would hear the deal.
On June the third retrial occurred, there still remained a hope.
A fail to score, Frank's last encore, would be upon the rope.
If luck played out, Frank had no doubt. His life was nearly through.
They'd beat one date, "The Pearly Gate," next July twenty-two.

Frank Williams had, for good or bad, been blessed with company.
And Alex Wood, for murder, stood convicted, first degree.
They'd ducked the hood, both Frank and Wood, on July twenty-two.
Two men condemned, by Satan hemmed; perhaps their lives were through.
Lum Nickerson, Ed Harrington, the third named Thomas Hughes;
Were all aboard for thefts occurred, confined to pay their dues.

Both Frank and Ed professed instead to vacate on the dot;
Thus thwart desire they be required to stay in jail and rot.
"If yea behoove to share the move, eliminate the tolls,
Friends, share this trip or we will rip your bodies from your souls."
When do or die the weak comply, what use to howl or weep?
Less forceful three did so agree, in fear the threat might keep.

Lum's wife and son had soon begun to languish at the jail.
The man beguiled his wife, with child, to raise four thousand bail.
Between them stood no likelihood they'd hustle half the cash.
This be the case, both time and place filled need for weapons stash.
The baby's shawl fit best of all, for secreting the arms.
So Emma came into the game, astride her infant's charms.

Caressed and smiled, Lum hugged the child, in daily ritual,
The time did come when guards ho-hum visits habitual.
This eased the mind of those inclined to relax frequently.
Soon Em' and Lum had overcome intent to oversee.
'Midst love, demure, guards felt secure. Lum's lawless days were done.

He leaned and smiled, then kissed the child, and palmed the hidden gun.

The deputy, a quid to free, brass cuspidor drew near.
Then when he spit a perfect hit, a pistol nudged his ear.
The jailer, Bill, was shaking still, when Lum possessed his keys.
Then Billy High reached for the sky, when Williams shouted, "Freeze!"
Deputy Hayes backed off a ways, then joined Bill in the jail.
The janitor made three the score, when bandits trimmed his sail.

Outside, the world still throbbed and whirled. Who dreamed what had evolved?
Bob Nickerson, Lum's father's son, shared brotherly resolve.
Beyond the square, grass grew like hair, providing means, of course.
To turn the wheels that clinched the deal, the entry of the horse!
One snorty mare Bob hobbled there, lest wanderlust impede.
The other two, young Robert knew, would be content to feed.

You see, indeed, Bob felt no need to join the crew in jail.
He failed to find, though taxed his mind, equipment for the trail.
He'd saddled one, but two wore none, except for ratty manes.
But gear amiss, they'd grasp at this, once shed those jail-house chains.
Poor Wood and Hughes (so sad the news) were left to flee afoot.
Two horses more, would show for sure, escape was at the root.

While, crooks inside were in full stride, the county treasurer,
To self-assure, approached the door of Bingham auditor.
Mr. Dineen, a guard, was seen to take his place aboard.
And Schuyler, John, the bailiff on the court, was not ignored.
With staff in jail, the chance to fail was lessened some degree.
The outlaw five sprang well alive, determined to be free.

Five helped themselves to sheriff's shelves, weapons upon the wall.
Their break, broad day', well under way, rejoicing freedom's call.
Armed to the teeth, killer and thief, so sudden bid adieu.
Enough of rest, became obsessed, their travels to renew.
With two horse thieves at Williams' sleeves, raced north to shake escort.
Hughes' venture scrapped when he was zapped, bound southward to "The Fort."

Woods played his card, searched for a pard to guide him on his way.
A red-skinned scout, a friend no doubt, appeared to save his day.
Through miles of sage, Wood drove Shank's Stage full hundred and a half.
Fortune did ride by stealth and stride; misfortune had its laugh.
His frantic hike to Golden Spike, did falter there and fail.
Forced to abort, rifle escort brought home to Bingham Jail.

Bob Nickerson, blamed for the run, secured his alibi.
Left hitched his steeds, "personal needs," involvement would decry.
His afternoon, he hoped, would prune all linkage to the crime.
He'd joined his pards to trump their cards and drink to good old times.
When Bob returned, his feigned concern was laced with grief and shock.
Remuda gone; he'd camp 'til dawn. 'Cause home was quite a walk.

Far up the trail did hoof-beats flail; des'prados taking flight
Had whipped and spurred, the three jail-birds went racing through the night.
Before the flock reached Eagle Rock, a message crackled forth.
Plans to delay had gone astray. Alert, by wire, went north.
Outlaw intent: trim to prevent the use of graphic wires.
A legal net, by splice, was set, a posse-manned backfire.

Behind the three, a wild melee had formed in hot pursuit.
Lawmen closed in, at risk of skin, each grim and resolute.
The outlaw band had not foreplanned escape so short of gear.
The bareback ride, to stay astride, caused chaffing of the rear.
This, you may know, did tend to slow the outlaws in their flight;
Somewhat subdued, sore pressed for food, were harried through the night.

At risk of harm, paused near Heath's farm, requesting rest and chuck.
Recess for naught, the first to spot: informed, Oliver Buck!
Two-hour delay had paved the way for Buck to fan the chase.
Good neighbors all honored the call. The hunt became the race!
Odds ten to one with smoking guns unsheathed to blaze away.
They'd closed the gap and sprung the trap by darkening of day.

Now thirty-five, air came alive with gunshots from the pack.
A four-mile flight lit up the night, laid bare the smoking track.
Ed Harrington, foot-shot by one ('twas he provoked the flight),
Still far from dead, but monoped, was tiring of the fight.
While bullets zinged the posse ringed Snake River's bushy banks;
It, crested so near overflow, would guard the outlaws flanks.

Out-gunned, out-manned, escape so banned defied the outlaw script.
On Tuesday morn', 'neath shouts of scorn, the posse's net was zipped.
Soon Brinson, Joe, stepped up the show, brushed out the bad-men three.
A ring of men had closed the pen, ending the hopeless spree.
All fight was gone by early dawn, holed up in drywash sands.
The murderer was most demure, and first to raise his hands.

INDICTMENT.

IN THE DISTRICT COURT OF THE 3rd JUDICIAL DISTRICT,
COUNTY OF Bingham TERRITORY OF IDAHO.

The People of the United States in the Territory of Idaho,

AGAINST

Frank Williams } ss.

In The District Court of the 3rd Judicial District in the County of Bingham May Term, A. D. 1887, Frank Williams is accused by the Grand Jury of the County of Bingham by this indictment of the crime of Murder committed as follows:

The said Frank Williams on the 17th day of December A. D. 1886, at the County of Bingham in the Territory of Idaho in and upon the body of one Winn, whose full name is to the Grand jurors aforesaid unknown, then and there being willfully, unlawfully, feloniously premeditatedly and of his malice aforethought did make an assault; and that the said Frank Williams with a certain axe which said axe he the said Frank Williams in both his hands then and there held, the said Winn in and upon the head of him the said Winn then and there willfully unlawfully feloniously premeditatedly, and of his malice aforethought did strike thrust penetrate and wound with the intent then and there him the said Winn willfully unlawfully feloniously premeditatedly and of his malice aforethought to kill and murder, giving to the said Winn then and there with the axe aforesaid in and upon the head of him the said Winn one mortal wound of which said with the intent then and there him the said Winn willfully unlawfully feloniously premeditatedly and of his malice aforethought to kill and murder, of which said mortal wound he the said Winn then and there at the time and place aforesaid instantly died And so the jurors aforesaid upon their oaths aforesaid do say that the said Frank Williams the said Winn in manner and form aforesaid willfully unlawfully feloniously premeditatedly and of his malice aforethought did kill and murder

Contrary to the form, force and effect of the statute in such cases made and provided, and against the peace and dignity of the people of the United States in the Territory of Idaho.

H C Harkness
Foreman of the Grand Jury

H. M. Bennett
District Attorney
Bingham County

Names of witnesses examined before the Grand Jury, on finding the foregoing indictment:

J. H. Bean
S. F. Taylor
Samuel Sibbett
Frank Glover

INDICTMENT.

The People of the United States

IN THE

TERRITORY OF IDAHO.

AGAINST

Frank Williams

V.

A TRUE BILL

H C Harkness
Foreman of the Grand Jury.

Presented by the Foreman of the Grand Jury, in the presence of the Grand Jury, in open District Court of the County of Bingham Territory of Idaho, and filed as a record of said Court this 4th day of May 1887

J. P. Voyle
Clerk.

Deputy Clerk.

By H. M. Bennett
District Attorney
Bingham County

Court Documents Courtesy Of The Bingham County Clerk's Office

Excited talk in Eagle Rock , down stream two dozen miles,
Kept lawmen's pride well satisfied, despite their haggard smiles.
Hungry and tired, were not inspired to make another bust,
Next break-out thrill they'd shoot to kill, for dead men you can trust!
So briefly free, the ruthless three returned to Taylor's jail;
Brought under guard, their sole reward, demand for strict servile.

Worn out by sport and tempers short, emotions bent and scarred,
They all had tracked, which one would act to claim the cash reward?
As talk grew loud, manners avowed recanting of the chase.
Though Brimson, Joe laid claim the dough, each filled a vital space.
A rule by court cut quarrel short before the trail grew cold.
The Judge decreed, each shared the deed, drew twenty dollars gold.

Several days, then Woods did raise his face among the crew.
All views allowed, seemed less than proud, acquaintance to renew.
No joys were shared, friendships repaired, adventures to report.
For two, at least, the chute was greased. There remained appeals court.
Williams and Woods, now understood, had one last ray of hope.
Shorter each day time swept away, and closer swung the rope.

Long weeks confined distorts the mind, for thought is but a seed.
Without fresh soil, productive toil, availed to fulfill need,
It atrophies and courts disease. Seed-beds become a grave.
When caged by cell, a living hell, morals are soon depraved.
In such a spot, constructive thought leans to the world outside.
Escape, no doubt, is tossed about, or even prophesied.

Frank sang that tune last year in June. The notes were rather brief.
Unlike before, another score may not end in grief.
If dealt the cards, he'd slay the guards, refuting hot pursuit.
Should foil the break, it could not make future more destitute.
This act was stilled, the beans were spilled, regards the murder plot.
To try, and fail, would prompt curtail each life-span with a shot.

In dreadful wait, Supreme Court date, Frank's fear was unconcealed.
"Appeal declined," addled his mind, at hopelessness revealed.
Not time for waste, a frantic haste engulfed to drive him wild.
Escape he'd steer, should chance appear, his plans yet uncompiled.
When law aborts all chance in court, the sentence stands for real.
Man's time aboard rests with his lord, a chance his soul to heal.

A second date: the noose awaits, next July twenty-one.

To save his face he'd lead the race, grab any chance to run.
Two weeks to live, lest fate should give an opportunity.
Chow-time, for life -- cook's carving knife held first priority.
To spite his head, guard sliced the bread, then placed the knife near by.
An accident for refuge meant, Frank made his final try.

The Sheriff's men relinquished then, their guns when faced the knife,
The guards, with ease, gave up the keys, when threatened with a life.
'Twas next the judge saw fit to budge, Shoemaker's choice -- a cell.
George Robethan, the audit man, escaped in time to tell.
Dashed through the door his office wore, he crashed the window pane.
His rousing shout, "They've broken out! They've all escaped again!"

Frank's right to live his all would give, not worth a dime a share.
He ducked and dove, through willows wove, like coyotes chase a hare.
The River Snake, if he could make its legendary shore,
'Twas wild, but hark, to last 'til dark required four hours or more.
And so he did, bushed up and hid, his freedom half that long;
Recapture fought until he's caught, to face his dreadful wrong.

Before nightfall had cast its pall across the prairie sage,
The birds who flew were trapped anew, to settle in their cage.
The pleasure trip destined to flip, before it ran its course;
Except for one, still free to run. Woods, somehow, gained a horse.
Dame Fortune spurned, was soon returned from north -- The Gallatin.
Woods missed the wreck that broke Frank's neck, but failed to save his skin.

Frank, to assure, would kill no more, came July twenty-one.
By hangman freed from misery, the killer's life was done.
Showed no remorse, with scant discourse, to spice his final day;
Who lives by gun, with mercy none, on gallows he must sway.
He's buried there, the courthouse square, that all concerned may know.
This final thought, got what he sought. Man reaps as he shall sow.

Keep trembling feet off Shilling Street, likewise its courthouse square.
Trespass the bold, for rumors hold, "A spirit wanders there."
He rides at night, cloud-filtered light, a writhing ghostly mass;
On lunar beams, a dream, it seems, a surging manshaped gas.
And some folks say, its head will sway, then nearly disconnect.
It twists and squirms like dying worms, when sunlight shines direct.
Not seen by day, what rumors say, considered on the brink.
It's thought they see Frank's fight to free his neck's immortal kinks.

Verdict

The People of the United States in the Territory of Idaho, against Frank Williams

Ind. No. 1.
For Murder

Now on this 31st day of May 1887 the District Attorney with the defendant and his counsel Willard Crawford Esq came into Court. The defendant was duly informed by the Court of the nature of the indictment found against him for the crime of murder committed on the 17th day of December 1886, of his arraignment, and plea of "not guilty as charged in the indictment" on the 4th day of May A.D. 1887, of his trial and the verdict of the jury on the 11th day of May A.D. 1887, "guilty of murder in the first degree." The defendant was then asked if he had any legal cause to show why judgment should not now be pronounced against him to which he replied that he had none and no sufficient cause being shown or appearing to the Court,

Now therefore the said defendant having been convicted of the Crime of murder in the first degree, It is hereby considered and adjudged that the said defendant Frank Williams be taken from the Court Room to the County Jail of Bingham County and from thence on the Twenty

Second Day of July A.D. One
Thousand Eight Hundred and
Eighty Seven, to the place of
execution and that he the
said Frank Williams there
between the hours of Twelve
o'clock M. and Four o'clock P.M.
of said day, be hung by the
neck until he is dead.

Death Certificate

Territory of Idaho } ss.
County of Bingham }

I hereby certify that I
executed the within warrant by reading
the same to the within named Frank
Williams at 1:55 P.M. o'clock and taking him
from the jail to place of execution
which I had prepared in the Court
House yard at Blackfoot the County
Seat of Bingham County, at 2 o'clock
P.M. and hanging him by the neck at 2:12 P.M.
on the 21st day of July 1888 and he
was pronounced dead by Dr. J.H.
Beam at 2:22 P.M.

J. F. Taylor
Sheriff of Bingham Co

AMBUSHED

Smoking down the asphalt trail, our thoughts were wheeling free;
Laying rubber trimmings north on U.S. 93.
The speed-valve on my "Jimmy" was buried to the shank,
She's belching smoke an' thunder, a tiger in her tank.

There's Loper riding shot-gun, like all the old hands do.
And we were plumb contented just to ride an' share the view.
The glint of winter sunlight brought comfort as we sped,
While smiling through the window in shades of gold an' red.

My eyes know what they're seeing, but how can this be true?
Those brilliant rays of sunshine were laced with blinking blue.
I gazed at this illusion, my jaw-bone hanging slack.
"Hot damn", said Loper, groaning,' "A trooper's on our track".

"Lope', see that sign out yonder, the limit's ninety-three.
No Idaho State Trooper makes a bumpkin outa me."
"Now button down", Lope' grumbled, "He'll make you walk the line.
That poster near the roadway's a U.S. highway sign."

I slowed my green crusader, then shut the motor down.
Ain't bowing to no trooper, just 'cause I came to town.
I offered this suggestion: "Hey, blue an' ped-ee-greed,
Your radar knows I'm driving within the legal speed."

"Look cowboy", growled the trooper, "You drop that sort of jive.
Your smoking 'Jimmy ' fliver can't muster thirty-five.
Now boys, a law's been written in journals of this state.
In most Judicial circles, it's called a license-plate."

"Now hold 'er, this brand's tallied in legal journals too.
How dare you claim my payment is two years over-due?"
I snatched my cache of papers an' offered up a batch;
But felt a weak sensation, the numbers didn't match!

While blushing like a lobster enshrined upon a plate;
"This paper's on a trailer, at home with my dear mate."
"The heat you're making, cow-poke, will only burn your stew.
You see, this trailer tally is also over-due!"

"Hey cop, I get the feeling this here's some sort of scheme.
And ev'ry thing I'm seeing is one psychotic dream."
When, humbled in composure, I flashed a second form,
To face the same reaction; I knew it wasn't norm'.

"Now rein-up, Sergeant Preston, you've had your little joke."
A third, and final, paper turned all my hopes to smoke.
My lips began to sputter, my jaw began to sag.
It's much too late for backing and humor ain't his bag.

"Now sir, I know your duty, but road-fines fluster me,
A bent an' broken cowboy, Alzheimer's is my plea."
The trooper thought his ticket should cure my mindless ways.
When I refused to pay it -- the judge said, "sixty days!"

I sit here contemplating on life before the car.
If I had traveled horse-back, this trail of rock an' tar;
The trooper, 'board a stallion, his posse at his side,
That brand not bein' proper -- they'd hang my bloomin' hide.

This poem is in appreciation of Idaho State Patrolman C.T. Rowland, a positive credit to law enforcement in Idaho.

CHRISTMAS AT GRANDMA'S

Since man's infinite wisdom blesses life so many ways,
Consider this: computers that encore the good old days.

Just punch a plastic button, put your worries on suspend.
Return, at will, to childhood, in a land of "let's pretend."
One could create a pageant, wherein lights glow from above.
And children act as angels, sanctifying acts of love.
With songs, and other angels, they become a Christmas choir,
Returning late to Grandma's, basking near a crackling fire.
They place home-crafted presents, as before, beneath the tree.
The gifts require endeavor, but the love inside is free.
On Christmas day the feasting, very often overdone,
And squeals of happy children serve to emphasize their fun.

The program does exist, friends, and like children's love, it's free.
Plug into your computer. Find it in the memory.

Never's a friend like yer old saddle hoss.
For sure, if you loose him it's been as great loss.
You learn, at such moments, yer heart is the boss.

THE GOOD LIFE

When hands of our creator over-blessed this rural space,
One thought needs no convincing: he designed a healing place,
For curling up the wrinkles most down-grading to the race;
By nurturing the senses 'til they realign the face.

He sprayed the country hillsides with a breath of mountain air;
Perfumed by countless flowers, eager each to do its share,
And all in brilliant colors like a rock musician's hair.
There is no human living who won't stop to gaze or stare.

He sprinkled miles of desert, quite befitting to its age,
With lavarock formations finely spiced with purple sage;
Where antelope and coyote lead a wildlife entourage,
Respecting tempting limits of their rock and sagebrush cage.

His silver creeks, all flowing from clear, percolating springs,
Feed moisture to the forest from wherein the songbird sings;
Providing peace and solace for a wealth of living things
And topping out the wonders that this regal splendor brings.

Consider now man's canyons, built of rock and window panes;
Black ranges topped in asphalt, that won't green-up when it rains
And decorated mountains bound by strings of passing lanes.
Give thanks that our designer kept us free of tar-topped chains.

Man makes his own selections from a host of pleasures rife,
Must be his own protector from a world of pain and strife.
Don't keep frustrations mounting, let them cut you like a knife.
Hit the trail to Idaho and try the cowboy life.

Harry Taylor In The Forties — Born A Cowboy

HARRY

Life has its share of treasures. From the heart is whence I speak;
Not always in the offing, though they're present if we seek.
I've thought back on life's livin' an' those many loyal friends,
Who come in several versions and in very special blends.
Some turn regret to pleasure but the pal is seldom found
With inborn cowboy humor tuned to'ard bending things around.
My old pal Harry Taylor fits, astoundingly, that niche,
His brand of homespun sayin's makes your funny-button click.

When we were gallivantin' down the road to earn our chuck;
I'd ply my brand of talent on rough horses known to buck.
One time I'd drawn a bad-one who'd right nearly had his way.
The "pick-up" came to save me from a floggin' by the clay.
I flipped my buck-rein to him and he caught it in a flash,
But missed his dally-welties and I ends up in a crash.
Har' says, "if you're enamored by some cute gal, sweet and grand,
Simply introduce yourself, then present to her your hand,
'Cause your attention-getters are much more than I can stand."

One time, in Old Montana, when I didn't "make" the trip,
There Harry stands, just grinnin' and a-givin' me this lip;
"Try to ride them longer, Bob, though I know he ain't your style,
The pay-off's always bigger if you stay aboard awhile.
I'm sure that both the judges are considerate an' kind,
But it might help them better if the two of them were blind."

When bad-draws had us busted an' it's Harry's turn to rope
And hunger seemed to fill him with both confidence an' hope;
Bending to'ard the serious he would drop his humored spiel,
Seek to feed the pair of us by loopin' of his veal.
Sometimes I'd get to dreamin' (chicken-dumplings in a pot);
Satisfaction realized, if per-chance his vealer's caught.
But if his cast, in failing, sails beyond his dogies eye;
"If I'd bought a shorter rope, he'd be smokin' 'neath muh tie."

One time, in Arizona, when we ain't been doin' well;
We're tired of eatin' nothin', to the point a job looks swell.
In search of better dinin' I'd plumb milked our grub-supply,
Made soup from dry frijoles, for to fortify our try.
Says Harry, "let's be searchin' our bare-naked pantry shelf.
That bean looks mighty lonesome, in there swimmin' by himself."

One night, just south of Denver, in a seedy little bar,

I overly committed to remove the bar-keep's tar.
Friend-Harry's in there helpin', well, he sorta set the bout ---
He called the man a booze-hound with male parentage in doubt.
The gent had granite knuckles and at least a dozen hands.
He finished going through me, while my pardner grins an' stands.
"Why didn't you just poke him, knock 'im down upon the sand?
Don't ever try to butt him. Learn to punch with either hand."

The hills of Old Wyoming aren't all peaceful as they seem.
For often times a brandin' might pursue an ardent dream,
To'ard bein' a cow baron, when the start is slow and lean.
There's men who have fulfilled it brandin' ev'ry head they seen.
Har's simple way of tellin' those acts that were transpirin',
"Them calves got burned an' branded sleepin on hot brandin' irons."

Those days are gone forever and we've weathered in their course.
Now we're both city dwellers who, but seldom, fork a horse.
Predestined is our future and our times may well be nigh.
Some place in timely distance we may journey to the sky.
I've never been right saintly so I'll take what fate inspires.
But I have no hankerin' for hell's hand-stoked brandin' fires.
Should I trek the higher road to that celestial town;
I'll find my old pard, Harry, garbed in white angelic gown,
Smokin' down the banister of that gilded, golden stair ---
But that won't fit his pistol, so he'll fit a cowboy flair
And dress for the occasion in red flannel underwear.

We lost Harry in 1995. There will never again be a dull
moment behind those pearly gates.

Cow-culture verse gives your life a free roll,
Curls up your lip-ends, and brightens your soul;
It won't always heal you but helps to console.

HOOTIE

My old pal, Freddy, met me
With a smile upon his face.
His beaming, glowing features
Showed more pride than social grace.
"Oh Pardner, please come with me,
You must meet my darling lass,
Her crowning beauty stuns me.
She is born of noble class."
So while his eyes they sparkled
Like two million dollar pearls,
My mind began to question,
"What of Sidney and the girls?"

His constant, ceaseless chatter
Beat like Tom Toms on my drums;
His eyes grew plump and reddish
Like two ripened sugar plums.
But these words they really caught me,
Set me fearing for his rep'.
He called her gaited travel,
"A hot, bouncing Spanish step."
His story left me speechless,
Though my mind performed in whirls.
My flabbergasted thinking
Pitied Sidney and the girls.

I'd think him less a bounder
If he'd but attempt to hide
Bold, scathing admiration
For "The way her footsteps glide."
Now all this time I'm thinking:
He must take me for a chump.
He sought for my approval
'Cause he loves to pat her rump.

I'm sure he never noticed
How my attitude he churls,
Diverting earned affection
From sweet Sidney and the girls.

He pumps his jaws and prattles
'Til I just can't help but stew.
He praised her looks "In halter,"
Says, "She's quite a thrill to view.
Her song is sweet and vibrant
In the early morning dew.
The hills ring back her echo
'Til it thrills me through and through.
She'd sing with no more beauty
If her vocal cords had curls.
It must sound more like braying
To dear Sidney and the girls.

"Her temper and composure,"
Freddy tells me right out flat,
"When blended with her posture
Makes a model Democrat.
Her royal lineage – top line –
Thereon Virgin Mary sat;
Her bottom, quarter breeding,
And say, ev'ry line could scat!"
My Lord, Fred's thoughts amaze me,
His head's a home for squirrels.
My heart's been truly bleeding,
But for Sidney and the girls.

Take that half-cast and stuff her.
Why you've made me out a fool --
With eyes lit up like fire-brands
And your trembling lips a-drool;
Tell me, how was I to know
Your love's a jenny mule?

Quote me if you'd like, old pard,
While your tale of lust unfurls.
You'd be a total cornball
But for Sidney and the girls!
Fred says, "Now hear my story:
Why your brains have gone and went.
And two cents for your thinking
Would be grossly over-spent.
How could the times we've been through
Leave you doubting my intent?
Just kiss my 'Royal Lass', Bob!
Take that as a compliment!"
I must control the anger
In my noggin as it twirls.
Though not berating Hootie,
I'll kiss Sidney and the girls!

    This is exactly the way Fred Hoopes called it. His passionate love affair with Hootie continues, but Sidney, Jenifer and Sarah tell me they are more emotional about her than is their respective husband and father .

THE BUTTON AND THE CHAMP
(POEM ONE OF A TRILOGY)

We both were reminiscing on the days that used to be,
Me and a champion rider who's a special friend to me.
We shared the pleasant mem'ries of the good old times we had,
When joys of life abounded; then we laughed about the bad.
He'd been acclaimed the champion of bull-riders back a way
And still a champ at fifty, he can make bull-riding pay.
Those years of bumps and bruises left their scars upon his hide
But that which keeps him winning is what's hid down deep inside.
The part exposed to viewing ain't the measure of the man,
Just see now what he looks like, in your mind's eye, if you can.

His gold emblazoned buckle proclaimed "Champion Of The World."
His boots were worn and battered and their toes were scuffed and curled.
Inspired by time were etchings, now engraved upon his face,
Like strips of it eroded when harsh winds whirled through the space.
His mustache drooped and wobbled like its tips were overweight.
He'd stand four inches taller if his legs had grown out straight.
Devoid of vegetation was the gloss upon his pate.
Most of it had died away or did not germinate.
His frame looked tough and wirey, like a wolf beyond its years,
But words of his achievements could have filled ten thousand ears.

A greenhorn spied the buckle with its golden glow of light
And promptly chose the moment for enrichment of his night.
He said, "I'm mighty anxious to meet such a famous hand,
Who's many times been touted as the greatest in the land."
The champ absorbed the tribute with a mirthless measured grin,
And pridefully admitted he's the best there's ever been.
The gods in all their fury could not his pride erase,
And bold determination framed the lines upon his face.
These words that button uttered cut his dollar to a dime:
"Now, Champ, will you please tell me, what was your fastest time?"

The Champ ignored the blunder, we all have made a few.
The moral to this story ain't what the button knew.
Now contemplate: each acorn may yield a mighty tree,

No man can tell, by looking, how hard its wood will be.
Who could expect a button, bare' facing change of voice,
 To question such profession in words that fit our choice?
The champ picked up the fumble in a way that prooved him grand,
Would not belittle someone who did not understand.
Instead he seemed to wriggle -- squirm down deeply in his hide,
And thus enhance the impact of the story of his ride.

The button gazed, enraptured, while this tale began to form,
Like a lost unshelterd mortal views a fierce approaching storm.
"One time in Californy, when I marked a ninety-three,
I crotched an ox named Snowman, belongin' to CB.
That three an' ninety markin' fairly scorched the judge's book.
You'd a thought I rode an earthquake, the way the grandstand shook.
I rode that ragin' demon an' we clearly stole the show,
That," said he, with misty eyes, "was thirty years ago,
But none could hold a candle to old Spec in sixty-one.
I rode to fame an' glory on that pitchin' Son-a-gun."

The Champ blinked off a tear drop in the corner of his eye,
Concluding for the button, complex ways of life and why.
His shoulders more erect now, and firmness in his step,
He told then of the basics for to build a button's rep'.
I could feel the bond of friendship reaching out between the two,
A warm and human welding of the old times to the new.
"Son, you'll be a champ perhaps, my time has come and went.
You must earn your niche in life, but you won't by accident.
Them that tries the hardest, son, only they will gain their choice,
For fame is not accomplished by mere raisin' of the voice."

Ronnie Rossen riding Spec in 1961 – Considered by many to be one of the all-time great bull rides.

RIDE FOR NINETY-ONE
(POEM TWO)

Free spoken words one yesteryear, before Punch journeyed on,
Left doubt to cloud our heart-to-heart: were bulls or we the pawn?
Through foamy glass time's bubbles passed from ev'ning into dawn.
The hours between exposed to me the hollow spot in Ron.

"A deed," says he, "impresses me, not windy, boastful words.
The testy Toros I've been through ain't found in dairy herds;
They add up like pulsing feathers in skies blocked out by birds.
I've never aimed to conquer them for seconds, fourths or thirds.

I beat the best I've ever seen, from Butler, Steiner, Todd.
I'd set my mind to get the bell, then take my wraps and nod.
I topped the greats the business owned, then dodged them — on the prod.
'Cause I never liked man-eaters a batterin' my bod'.

But there's one last goal remaining — forever tempting me.
I scored a ninety-one on Spec... Snowman earned ninety-three.
Spec always was the tougher ox so he's the goal you see.
My pride lacks one more ninety-one to let my soul fly free."

So Punch faced his great obsession, determined he'd not fail;
Hand-warmed the rope and nod the head, beware the greasy tail.
A hoof, a horn, unplanned abort -- abruptly ends the trail,
A rip instead, a gush of red, a cowboy's face turned pale.

God penned his epitaph in full before the day was done.
The final score on Ron's last ride - a blazing ninety–one.
 Punch fulfilled his great ambition. The life-long race was run —
One balmy autumn afternoon ... The year was ninety-one!

THE LONG RIDE
(POEM THREE)

I was horseback on "The Blackfoot"
When a flutter turned my eye
To the curious contortions
Of a form up in the sky.
Then a twirling apparition
Angled upward on the fly.
I was rendered cold and breathless
And my mouth turned powder dry.

First the sunlight bobbed and flickered,
Like its bulb was burning out.
Then it cast an eerie shadow,
Though there were no clouds about.
In that swirling, whirling madness
I could bare restrain a shout.
Though the day looked warm and cheery,
I could feel the goose-bumps sprout.

My old horse's nostrils quivered
Then he whistled blasts of air,
While a frenzy of emotion
Seemed to leap from everywhere;
In an atmosphere so heavy
I could almost chew the air.
Though it ain't this cowboy's custom --
I knelt in silent prayer.

Then that cyclone of confusion
Seemed to melt into the sun;
While the day turned sudden Pleasant --
As before this all was done.

When my pulse returned to normal
I had lost the urge to run;
But my mind still raced on blindly
As a bullet from a gun!
When I heard the story later
Why I bowed my head and cried;
While weird tangles of emotion
Pricked like brambles 'neath my hide.
It was not a dusty hillside,
Where you made your final ride;
But upwards to the heavens,
For I saw you pass inside.

Most of life's pleasures are humble indeed,
Especially for cowboys and folks of their breed.
I can't grant you pleasure but here is the seed.

TOM, DO YOU REMEMBER?

Tom, do you remember what your mother used to say?
"All the cain you're raising will come back to haunt some day."
Tom, you might remember, as you read my simple rhymes;
When our lives are toughest, we recall the good old times.

Tom, do you remember all the impishness of youth?
You were pulling "funnies" by the time you grew a tooth.
Tom, do you remember raiding Igor Johnson's coop
Of his fattest pullet, which was roasted by the group?

Tom, do you remember? It was just a boyish lark;
Flames engulfed the outhouse, while you puffed on Cedar bark.
Tom, do you remember how pa raked you through the coal —
Forced to use the neighbor's 'cause you'd burned the fam'ly hole?

Tom, do you remember getting plowed on Devil's Brew?
You'd have fought a lion after downing more than two.
Tom, do you remember when you couldn't find your bed?
Woke up there beside it, sleeping on the floor instead.

Tom, do you remember when you neutered that stray pup,
Quelled his lusty romance 'cause he over-ran his cup?
Tom, do you remember Aunty Bessy's pusy cat?
You used paint remover, you said, "Teach her how to scat!"

Tom, do you remember when you flunked a math exam.,
'Cause you'd been playing hooky and just didn't give a damn?
Tom, do you remember all the fun you had in school?
In your quest for humor you forgot the golden rule.

Tom, do you remember when the bull steam-rollered John--
Not the least respectful of his courage or his brawn?
Tom, do you remember when bronc-peeling was our game?
All those cowboy antics did not carve our niche in fame.

Tom, do you remember when you told Bernice those lies,

Things you contemplated as you looked into her eyes?
Surely you remember, now you're paying for the deed.
See how your romancing brought a wife and kids to feed.

Sure Tom, you remember what your mother used to say.
And the cain you raised then surfaced in another way.
Tom, we both have mem'ries, age makes them sweeter too.
Bless that cane, old pardner, 'cause now it's raising you.

My old college buddy, Tom Farrington, suffered a severe stroke a few years ago. I wrote, and sent to him, the above poem. This wasn't intended as an accusation but there could be enough truth in it to assist in the returning of that impish grin to Tom's face.
 Bernice reports: "The cane is still raising Tom."

I hope you enjoy this plain country verse.
Though poetry bugs may strike like a curse,
Life's like a horse-trade; You might have done worse.

THE JAM O'R JERRY'S ROCK

The penchant for peace or adventure,
Oft' born of municipal wedge,
The hum-drum and strife of our culture,
Push hard-driven souls to the edge.
A lifetime of toil and self-torment
Helped etch the deep lines on my brow
Thus setting the place and the moment
For the tale I'm telling you now.

Our hearts and our heads seeking pleasure,
We paused for a trek through the woods,
Where rest and relaxation measure
Much greater than store-purchased goods.
We planned for a few days of splendor,
Like nature alone can provide,
We'd no thought in mind but surrender
To solace and beauty and pride.

Pack horses were laden and tethered
With diamond-tied twist of the rope.
The wilderness, rugged and weathered,
Exceeded the reach of our hopes.
There's Jerry, aboard his top rope-mare,
And Dexter, a-straddle his best.
Both Nipper and Red Flag I'd brought there,
A-trailing behind all the rest.

We drank in the optical wonders,
The crags reaching out to the sky.
Cool, clear, trickling streams of fresh water
Beguiled us as we drifted by.
The track of the elk and the bob cat
Looked up from the trail where we rode.
Crossing the wild creatures door mat,
We entered their gorgeous abode.

An ash-blackened stump made us wonder...
Cremated by heat from the blast,
When the heavens, pregnant with thunder,
Threw flames in the arrows they cast.
Inspired by its beauty, commanding,
So smitten by nature's fine brush,
Blissfully slow we responded,
As the sun arced west with a blush.

Come evening, our training domestic
Of practical life less than best,
Abated our viewing majestic,
Turning thoughts to forage and rest.
Invading a lush forest grassland.
Abundant with feed it was blessed,
A spreading, green emerald island,
With diamond-like spring at its breast.

A reclining hulk of down-timber,
Magnificent though death-depressed,
Now framing the wilderness picture,
Was lying , in state, to the west.
For nature, still blessing our outing
With symbols of beauty and might,
Provided, without further scouting,
This rack for our saddles that night.

It seems as if nature's fine balance
Hangs trembling on fine silken threads.
The peace of a wonderland palace
May quickly be rendered to shreds.
Emotion restricts full compliance
When ropes limit horses at feed.
Though you think you've wrought an alliance,
Don't place all your bets on the steed.

True, hindsight enlightens beholders,
But calms not the brain of the beast.

I'd picketed Flag to a boulder,
In doing, reflex action greased...
Erasing his trust for all mankind,
And limiting rational thought.
When coil-springs of rope fore-legs entwined,
Mind-blinded by terror he fought.

When we paused to dwell on the notion
To "tent up" and lay out our beds,
Red Flag, with a desperate motion,
Whirled, bucking and fighting his head.
Our camp fairly popped with excitement,
Though nature still glowed with aplomb,
So frenzied was Red Flag's deportment,
He blew like the burst of a bomb.

I treasure the thrill of such moments,
A poet his lifetime would give.
His thoughts are oft' burdened with torment,
To write a few verses that *live*!
Now , gaze upon this mental picture
Of Flag, bearing down at full speed,
A bounding rock chasing the creature,
Increasing his urge to be freed.

With haste geared by madness, not planning,
Flag zeroed his race in on me.
To keep him from more country spanning,
I dallied the root of that tree.
All furious effort was failing,
An end to his flight not to be.
He jerked the rope slack and was flailing,
Roots shattered and chaos reigned free.

'Twas then we felt a foreboding,
The shock in our minds turned to dread.
Gone loco, Flag's frantic exploding
Made Jer' miss his pass at the head.
But Jer', with athletic endeavor,

Then straddled the rope on the fly.
Flag, making his run to forever,
Showed torrents of fear in his eye.

You'll fathom the total confusion,
But never envision the shock.
It certain was not a delusion,
Caught Jer' in the tail, 'twas the rock.
Over there, in "Bonny Ald England,"
They'd call it a *great* steeple chase.
The rock, with poor Jerry aboard it,
Was rapidly leaving the place.

'Tis, often a cool summer evening,
One dwells on the visions that are.
Some, close to the heart, may cause grieving,
While others inspire from afar.
And, sometimes, the heavens look very
Much like a great shower of stars.
If so, it's that rock and poor Jerry,
Sparks trailing them skyward to Mars.

AN ODE TO JERRY

Now Jer', that's enough of those antics,
So swap ends. Please turn Flag around.
'Cause heaven won't welcome your antics.
Just park yourself here on the ground.
But if you feel up to an encore,
Don't waste such a good rodeo,
There's no time to search for a sponsor.
We'll film you for home video.

Ask Dexter Douglas about it. Jerry Jensen flatly refused us, and continues to do so to this very day.

LOSS BREEDS LONESOME

Sure leaves a feller lonesome
  When a pardner drifts away
From weathered boots and saddle
  That were filled just yesterday.

His top hoss, ears pricked forward,
  Focus on the window pane,
Searching long for Grandad,
  With his daily bait of grain.
Blue waits outside and whimpers;
  He knows not what is wrong.
Pop always drove the pickup
  So his Blue could ride along.

Three short days 'til brandin',
  Can't you smell the burning hair?
That firm hand on the iron...
  God, I wish he could be there!
He never missed a tally
  When the herd rushed out to grass,
Made sure the calves all mothered
  'Fore the daylight hours would pass.

His sparkle truly brightened
  The domestic side of life.
The warmth spent on his charges
  Clearly doubled for his wife.
The kids and fam'ly members?
  Just count their many tears.
They well exceed the tally
  He kept those many years.

Sure leaves a feller lonesome
  When a pardner drifts away
From weathered boots and saddle
  That he filled, just yesterday.

THE MAVERICK BULL

Lush grass applauds the mountain's crest,
Where trees appeal to heaven's breast,
And fresh-air breeds a life-long zest,
For life in the intriguing West.

Pure, blue lakes sparkle, cattle roam,
White bellies wrap from tail to dome,
'Round auburn frames ... kindred from home,
A shining herd of bovine chrome.

I felt a shock, intense surprise,
Strange, mottled colors caught my eyes.
Those calves had horns twice normal size...
All proper breeding this belies.

The change of hue, horns half an ear...
A problem does exist, I fear.
The answer rang out bold and clear.
Amour had caused some changes here.

My scientific breeding plan
Was led awry by beast or man.
It mattered not, I'd sought to ban
The strains that through my herd now ran.

The choice was clear: to map a course,
Then mount my toughest roping horse,
Remove this mystic, changing force,
Before the symptoms grow still worse.

Then on the roughest range I own,
Spied this old maverick, hide and bone,
With breeding like I'd never known,
And scabby back the flies had blown.

A lesser bull was never bred...
A living symbol of the dead.
His eyes, a mattered, hate-filled red,
Peered back at me, as off he sped.

He's hideous of head and horn;

His scraggly form alluding scorn,
Bucked in the knees, hooves long but worn,
With scars from whence dew claws were torn.

The spattered feces on his trail
Was scattered by his hocks and tail.
To match his haste o'r hill or dale,
A mountain goat himself would fail.

The summer faded, time moved on.
Each ridge I crossed I'd find him gone.
I trailed the useless bovine spawn,
Both night an' day, at dusk or dawn.

I rode his track through pine and spruce.
Attempts to shake me were no use.
I bottomed out my spent cayuse,
Then caught another, turned him loose.

The old bull's speed defied his age.
I tracked him on, through rocks and sage.
But when I thought him ripe to cage,
He'd up and write another page.

Who wins success, failure defies.
The sprint through life, one lives or dies.
Enduring all this tale implies,
I roped him deep below the eyes.

Afraid to miss... jerked in the slack,
Then laid it neatly o'r his back,
Spun safe three dallies on my kack,
An' dropped him like a rifle's crack.

I sought to end his beastly lust,
Prepared to void the brute I'd cussed.
Then, toe-to-toe the scoundrel trussed.
I'd leave him there to rot and rust.

I thought about this grizzly moose,
How he'd outrun my best cayuse
Through sage and miles of Mountain Spruce,
Then scalped his pride and cut him loose.

LUCK

Life will test a cowboy
  When bad luck plays a round.
Some abusive cases
  may perforate the ground.
Those of stalwart mettle
  Won't change by act or sound.
They bear down and hustle
  'Til good luck does abound.

LIGHT THE BOARD

We can best assess a horse race when the photo is in hand.
The greying at our temples helps us each to understand
That those who may search backward through the hazy mist of years
Must base their final judgement on the picture that appears.
We leave the track a winner, if we live by this accord:
Being first is less important if we can but light the board.

If the track is poorly bladed, being such that going's rough,
The fact is, though it hinders, it won't ever stop the tough.
With thunder a crescendo, rain is gushing down the track
While lightning flashes brightly as a spot light on the back.
The stretch turns wet and slippery; what's the best we can afford?
Just rise up in those irons, beat the odds and light the board.

I bought a fragile yearling 'cause I got her for a song.
I figured that I'd feed her 'til a buyer came along.
I felt I'd bought a looser so to keep her wasn't hard.
The day she won her maiden she was there to fill the card.
She had not speed, but courage, for she would not be ignored.
She gutted up and won it; I'd just hoped she'd light the board.

From then on little "Hard Luck" was the darlin' of the crowd;
Of sheer determination, how much is a horse allowed?
When cash-flow turned so dismal I could barely stay abreast,
Why, Hard Luck seemed to sense it, and she ran her mortal best.
You give an inch she'd take it, while the fans rose up and roared.
She'd light, while tears flowed freely, the top line on the board.

I brought my new fiance out to meet the flat track crowd,
All puffed up like a rooster when he's crowing, shrill an' loud.
Expecting to be greeted by a chiding from the boys,
We eased up to the paddock with no fanfare and no noise.
Old Sam, the racing steward, looked her over like he's bored,
Then met my eye just beaming. He said, "Son, you've lit the board."

I don't recall a question ... Said, "I'd like it if you'd stay."

We paired up from that moment, double harness all the way.
Then came to bless us, children, just a fam'ly, not a crowd;
They proved life's greatest pleasure, reinforced our feelings proud.
No shade of doubt may cloud it, it's a win however scored,
And team-work is the reason, love will always light the board.

Each story has an ending. There's a close to ev'ry day.
However sweet the fiddle, there shall come a time to pay.
I haven't built my lifetime on the Scriptures as implored,
But neither have I faltered when I gave a man my word.
When God rings down the window, and he pops that final gate,
I don't expect an angel choir to pluck their harps in wait.
I ask no satin cooler from the household of The Lord,
I'll feel I'm well received there if I rise to light the board.

You won't find good humor each place that you look,
By prodding your pardner or maybe the cook,
But less flack will fly if it comes from a book.

To marry for money, ah yes, that's a gambit;
The truth of the matter: you damned well might earn it.

Paul Scott on Poco Rojo. Note the ribbon in his pocket.

UNCLE PAUL

Pro-Rodeo needed "The Turtles," wrought by cowboys "who stuck out their necks,"
Defying the greedy promoters skimming mostly cash-entries from checks.
Yes, he was a young charter member joining others in lengthy debate.
The power enjoined by sheer numbers put more beans on the poor cowboy's plate.

Then soon came equine reconstruction, laying cayuse and remount to rest.
"King Ranch", convinced cowboys who ride them, that a Quarter Horse fit them the best.
Once more to the fore of the challenge, facing doubts from a treasure of friends,
He drove from the state of potatoes into Prescott, to lead off the trend.

Our faith in the man did not vanish, for he broke to the lead of the pack.
And I, still a kid, gazed in wonder of two stallions he chose to bring back.
Though Coon Dog was small, he was mighty – wisely bred (in the purple) for speed.
His stable-mate, named Poco Rojo, was a rope-horse with prepotent seed.

Up-grading by these Quarter Stallions changed the Idaho horse overnight.
And prospects for two handsome horses were growing increasingly bright.
The strength of genetic improvement was fulfilling a widening need.
Match-racing and contested roping helped a risky adventure succeed.

Reflecting a great love for horses and the western traditions he knew,
Amazingly, no one predicted that he'd buy out the old "Flying U."[1]
Warm-hearted respect from a horseman, for the outlaws few men choose to ride
Is the ultimate proof of his greatness and the spirit he harbored inside.

Hats off to a crusty old cowboy, a legend who's played out his time.
He tackled the world with bold gusto when he owned not the worth of a dime.
Requiring a huge man to fill them are the boots he is leaving behind.
Join me in a moment of silence. We are losing the last of his kind!

[1] *Flying U Rodeo Company: Purchased from J.C."Doc" Sorenson by Uncle Paul Scott and later, resold to Dick Pasco & Cotton Rosser. Dick later sold out his share to Cotton.*

SOCK IT TO HER AL

We camped beside a meadow green...
Most pleasant valley ever seen,
Where coyotes yip and eagles preen,
Me and my pals from Jackson.

A creek-side camp would ease our drouth
And catch the sun rays from the south.
We'd rest our tails, abuse our mouths,
While showing little action.

Sometimes we'd rise up off our spines
Enough to wet our fishing lines;
Or maybe wander though the pines...
To varied satisfaction.

Our horses grazing near the trail
Would stamp a foot or switch a tail,
Consume the oats left in a pail,
And suffer no distraction.

One day six horses read the breeze,
Then hit the back-trail through the trees,
They left us foot loose, if you please,
To face unknown infraction.

An old she bear that cut our trail
Had put our horses under sail.
She made the three of us turn tail
And set our boots to scratchin'.

She licked her lips and ate her way
Through all the grub we'd left that day,
Then put our camp in disarray;
We three still seeking traction.

Just then we heard a frightful groan.

That bear began to roar and moan...
'Bout like a fog horn overblown,
Her ribs racked in contraction.

She grasped her belly with her paws.
A frenzy racked her dripping jaws.
She met her death, who'd guess the cause,
In moments, less a fraction.

We watched from high up in the rocks.
Her course of action reason blocks.
She'd eaten Allen's dirty socks
An' died of gas compaction.

I don't expect my good friend, Allen Raver, to admit his involvement in the chain of events described herein and I wouldn't tell the story if I hadn't caught him placing a pair of "Tenny Runners" in his saddle bags, as we were preparing to depart the trailhead (They were yellow Tenny Runners). I asked him why he was including "Walking Tools" in his gear when we were going for an extended HORSEBACK RIDE.

He said, "Bob, I'm taking them along just in case we run into a bear."

"Allen, You can't outrun a bear, no matter what you wear on your feet," I replied, with a considerable amount of disgust.

Then he flashed one of those, I got you that time, grins and, still wearing it, he replied, "I don't have to outrun the bear, Bob. I only have to outrun you!"

Author Bob Schild — Serious About This Bull!
Riverside, California 1958

RODEO JUDGE

His "John B." [1] reflected the old "Turtle" days,
Straight up in the middle an' dented four ways.
His boots, worn an' scrufty, were starving for care.
Jack Frost, it appeared, had high-lighted his hair.
Curled, top from bottom, the Wranglers he wore,
Rose outward then inward, like tusks of a boar.

Containing a quid, while it pickled his mouth,
He tight-lipped an accent born somewhere down south.
"Not cunning nor crafty shall make me a fool.
Ah'm sharp as a razor, mah brain mah best tool.
Ah'd lak to jine up with yoe oh-h-ficials pool.
That's why Ah've applied fo' thuh pro-judges school."

"Ah'm wild, boys, and wooly, fo' sure Ah ain't green.
Ah've performed in places you pups never seen.
Ah've mingled with culture, whooped up on the mean,
Knowed purty slim pickin's when times has growed lean.
Ah've cajoled with floozies, broke bread with a queen,
In slums, one stone castle, an diggin's between."

" Ah'm coldly perceptive. Ah speak mah own mind,
More mean than a badger, the wust of my kind.
No point's wuth contendin', don't cry, cheat nor fudge.
Who tries me cain't buy me. Ah ain't gonna budge.
When tempers git nasty, I don't hold no grudge.
Ah'm perfectly honed fo' tuh be a good judge!"

"Thar's some won't bulieve me, thuh hand thet Ah am.
Wall, put plain an simple, Ah don't give a damn!
Past friendships cain't bend me so let ut be said,
Y'all best come a shankin' when yew nod yoe head.
Last but not least, mah best feature y'all find,
Completin' thuh package – Ah'm totally blind!"

[1] John B. Stetson, Western Hat

GRACIAS AMIGOS

Unseen friends who read this book,
While curled in some secluded nook,
Share more than time required to look.

As you've lingered o'r my script,
Or briefly through its pages skipped,
My wish: A pleasant smile you've lipped.

If my pen has fired no blanks,
Instead, sends chuckles through your ranks,
I've reached my goal . Most sincere thanks!

                                            From:

                                  Author: Bob Schild
                                  Illustrator: Mike Stanger

ORDER FORM

SPUR TRACKS & BUFFALO CHIPS

Cowboy Verse and Country Chortling
$9.95 + tax and $1.50 Postage & Handling

PURE BULL -WELL ORGANIZED

Cowboy Poetry, Folklore and Western History
$11.95 + tax and $1.50 Postage & Handling

Both Books *Plus* Folding Cowhide Leather Case
Durable Foldover Case Suitable For Carrying In Saddlebags, Automobile, Etc.
$37.50 + tax and $3.00 Postage & Handling

Send check or money order to: B Bar B Leather
719 W. Pacific
Blackfoot, ID 83221

_____ Spur Tracks & Buffalo Chips _____
Quantity   Amount

_____ Pure Bull -Well Organized _____
Quantity   Amount

_____ Both Books *Plus* Leather Carrying Case _____
Set(s)   Amount

Total Enclosed _____
Please Allow 4 to 6 Weeks For Delivery
Immediate Delivery with Certified Check or Money Order

SHIP TO: _____
NAME

_____
ADDRESS (OR P.O. BOX)   APT. #

_____
CITY   STATE   ZIP

PLEASE PRINT LEGIBLY THIS WILL BE USED AS THE MAILING LABEL FOR YOUR PURCHASE

ORDER FORM

SPUR TRACKS & BUFFALO CHIPS

Cowboy Verse and Country Chortling
$9.95 + tax and $1.50 Postage & Handling

PURE BULL -WELL ORGANIZED

Cowboy Poetry, Folklore and Western History
$11.95 + tax and $1.50 Postage & Handling

Both Books *Plus* Folding Cowhide Leather Case
Durable Foldover Case Suitable For Carrying In Saddlebags, Automobile, Etc.
$37.50 + tax and $3.00 Postage & Handling

Send check or money order to: B Bar B Leather
719 W. Pacific
Blackfoot, ID 83221

_____ Spur Tracks & Buffalo Chips _____
Quantity   Amount

_____ Pure Bull -Well Organized _____
Quantity   Amount

_____ Both Books *Plus* Leather Carrying Case _____
Set(s)   Amount

Total Enclosed _____

Please Allow 4 to 6 Weeks For Delivery
Immediate Delivery with Certified Check or Money Order

SHIP TO: _____
NAME

_____
ADDRESS (OR P.O. BOX)   APT. #

_____
CITY   STATE   ZIP

PLEASE PRINT LEGIBLY THIS WILL BE USED AS THE MAILING LABEL FOR YOUR PURCHASE